React Native Cookbook
Bringing the Web to Native Platforms

Jonathan Lebensold

2018.

Beijing · Boston · Farnham · Sebastopol · Tokyo   O'REILLY®

React Native Cookbook

by Jonathan Lebensold

Published by O'Reilly Media, Inc., 1005 Gravenstein Highway North, Sebastopol, CA 95472.

O'Reilly books may be purchased for educational, business, or sales promotional use. Online editions are also available for most titles (*http://oreilly.com/safari*). For more information, contact our corporate/institutional sales department: 800-998-9938 or *corporate@oreilly.com*.

Editors: Nan Barber and Meg Foley
Production Editor: Kristen Brown
Copyeditor: Kim Cofer
Proofreader: Christina Edwards

Indexer: Judith McConville
Interior Designer: David Futato
Cover Designer: Karen Montgomery
Illustrator: Rebecca Demarest

March 2018:   First Edition

Revision History for the First Edition
2018-02-13:   First Release

See *http://oreilly.com/catalog/errata.csp?isbn=9781491993842* for release details.

978-1-491-99384-2

[LSI]

Table of Contents

Preface

When my first React Native application landed on the App Store, I knew the folks behind this technology were onto something special. At the time, I had only spent a few days working with the iOS ecosystem and found myself overwhelmed with Xcode, Objective-C, and the libraries for iOS. My last foray into iOS development was almost 8 years ago and, with a background in web development, I was intimidated. I also knew there were lots of others in the same boat.

React Native changed all of this overnight. I found myself at home with a design philosophy and set of skills I had developed as a web application developer. Better still, my app wasn't going to be a second-class citizen. I can't stand rigid animations and clumsy scrolling. React Native is an open source toolset that brings native application development to the countless JavaScript developers the world over.

Who Should Read This Book

You are already familiar with programming and JavaScript in particular. This book assumes you are tackling common software design choices that arise when building native applications. You may be working in your garage on the next great social media platform, or turning a lumbering enterprise system into a zippy mobile experience. If you're trying to bring a cross-platform native application to market quickly and have chosen React, this book is for you. Every section of the book is rooted in personal experiences building native applications.

Why I Wrote This Book

There is a ton of information online about React Native: the documentation is plentiful, and between StackOverflow and the React Native issues on GitHub, you will be able to solve most discrete programming problems. This book tries to go a little deeper: how do you organize a project? How can you design a user experience that accounts for asking users for permission to use their camera? These are common questions that require some thought and don't necessarily have one solution. This is a cookbook: the recipes should provide a great starting point. Let them inspire you to come up with your own solutions, or produce something when you're in a pinch!

A Word on JavaScript Today

It feels like every week JavaScript reinvents itself with a new name, a new set of language features, and new transpilers and compilers! Whether you call it ECMAScript, ES6, ES6+, or find yourself transpiling from TypeScript, CoffeeScript, NativeScript, Flow, Elm, or Reason, the ultimate output runs on a JavaScript virtual machine. *JavaScript fatigue* is real: with so much movement, how do you stay focused on a stable set of technologies?

There is no right answer. Know that all of these tools are simply trying to make you, the software developer, more productive. If these conditions are satisfied, then you should sleep well at night knowing that when the next wave crashes, you will be in the company of a supportive open source community preparing to catch the undercurrent. For the purposes of this book, I use the terms JavaScript and ES6 interchangeably. In the final section, I challenge you to embrace this shifting landscape by studying how the same component written in ES6 can be rewritten with Reason, a functional programming language built on top of OCaml!

Navigating This Book

This book is organized into six chapters:

- Chapter 1 discusses JavaScript tools and how they work with React Native.
- Chapter 2 explores the React Native ecosystem: how you leverage what is available and how to bring it into your project.
- Chapters 3 and 4 go into some common challenges seen in most applications: handling application state, dealing with device I/O, and structuring your design assets.
- Chapter 5 describes the deployment process and some techniques for reducing your delivery time.
- Chapter 6 tackles writing maintainable code: making code reusable, portable, self-documenting, and adding tools that catch bugs before your customers do.

Like any cookbook, it's best to flip through the examples and see how they connect with the work you are trying to accomplish. If you are already familiar with React Native or feel at home with Node, NPM, and Yarn, I suggest skipping Chapter 2. If you have already written native applications, then Chapter 1 is probably worth flipping through.

Online Resources

React Native relies on a suite of tools that can be loosely grouped into three categories: JavaScript tools, Apple SDKs, and Android SDKs. React Native bundles all your code into a JavaScript bundle that then runs on the native platform (for example, Android or iOS). Ensure these native platforms are installed correctly by following the React Native Getting Started guide (*http://bit.ly/2GWQDfo*).

If you have no experience with React, the React Overview (*http://bit.ly/2nIA4vr*) should help you stay oriented. I recommend looking through some of these references before starting this book. This list touches on a collection of technologies that underpin much of the React Native developer experience, including JavaScript/ES6, NPM, React, React Native, and Redux:

- The definitive guide: React Native: Getting Started (*http://bit.ly/2GWQDfo*)
- A quick primer on the transpiler powering our JavaScript pipeline: Learn ES2015 (*http://bit.ly/2nJb1Z8*)
- A great introduction to the Node Package Manager (NPM): What is npm? (*http://bit.ly/2EalFyf*)
- An excellent and concise explanation of React: React Overview (*http://bit.ly/2nIA4vr*)
- A community directory of all things React Native: Awesome React Native (*http://bit.ly/2EoLga3*)
- Free video tutorials discussing state management by the creator of Redux: Getting Started with Redux (*http://bit.ly/2ENagFH*)
- A curated directory of React Native packages: Opinionated catalog of Open Source React Native packages (*https://native.directory*)
- A listing of React Native packages available via NPM: An open catalog of React Native libraries (*http://bit.ly/2E8wuRF*)

Conventions Used in This Book

The following typographical conventions are used in this book:

Italic
> Indicates new terms, URLs, email addresses, filenames, and file extensions.

`Constant width`
> Used for program listings, as well as within paragraphs to refer to program elements such as variable or function names, databases, data types, environment variables, statements, and keywords.

Constant width bold

Shows commands or other text that should be typed literally by the user.

Constant width italic

Shows text that should be replaced with user-supplied values or by values determined by context.

This element signifies a tip or suggestion.

This element signifies a general note.

This element indicates a warning or caution.

O'Reilly Safari

 *Safari* (formerly Safari Books Online) is a membership-based training and reference platform for enterprise, government, educators, and individuals.

Members have access to thousands of books, training videos, Learning Paths, interactive tutorials, and curated playlists from over 250 publishers, including O'Reilly Media, Harvard Business Review, Prentice Hall Professional, Addison-Wesley Professional, Microsoft Press, Sams, Que, Peachpit Press, Adobe, Focal Press, Cisco Press, John Wiley & Sons, Syngress, Morgan Kaufmann, IBM Redbooks, Packt, Adobe Press, FT Press, Apress, Manning, New Riders, McGraw-Hill, Jones & Bartlett, and Course Technology, among others.

For more information, please visit *http://oreilly.com/safari*.

How to Contact Us

Please address comments and questions concerning this book to the publisher:

O'Reilly Media, Inc.
1005 Gravenstein Highway North
Sebastopol, CA 95472
800-998-9938 (in the United States or Canada)
707-829-0515 (international or local)
707-829-0104 (fax)

We have a web page for this book, where we list errata, examples, and any additional information. You can access this page at *http://bit.ly/reactNativeCookbook*.

To comment or ask technical questions about this book, send email to *bookquestions@oreilly.com*.

For more information about our books, courses, conferences, and news, see our website at *http://www.oreilly.com*.

Find us on Facebook: *http://facebook.com/oreilly*

Follow us on Twitter: *http://twitter.com/oreillymedia*

Watch us on YouTube: *http://www.youtube.com/oreillymedia*

Acknowledgments

Thanks to all the reviewers of this book: Spencer Carli, Matt Hamil, and Arnar Þór Sveinsson. Their insights and technical feedback on a fast-changing ecosystem gave me added confidence in the material included in this book. I take full responsibility for the content of the book, but it would have been much less readable without their suggestions.

This book would not have been possible without the Paradem team, particularly my cofounder Kevin Pratt, who made it possible for me to focus on writing. I am also grateful to Ezra Hopkins, Scott Luetke, and Abdullah Norozi, who were on hand as I was working through the chapters. Scott Schaffter and Jay Perry at Bivee Inc. provided me with the inspiration and encouragement to keep writing. Thank you O'Reilly Media, and particularly Nan Barber, for offering feedback and guiding the publishing process.

I would like to thank Facebook for sharing React Native with the world. I am also grateful to the folks in the Reactiflux Discord server for offering tech support, particularly with Reason. I am most thankful to all the individuals and organizations who are contributing their knowledge and source code with the open source community.

Lastly, I wish to thank my loving wife, Tara, for cheering me on and providing thoughtful insights.

CHAPTER 1

The React Native Toolchain

React Native lives in an ecosystem with dozens of little software tools. You have transpilers (Babel, Metro, Webpack), package managers (NPM, Yarn), linters, unit test frameworks, and more. This chapter will cover the language basics and the minimum set of open source tools you will be working with in your React Native project. You're probably writing your React Native application with JavaScript or some kind of transpiled source that compiles down to JavaScript, like TypeScript or ES6+. I hope this chapter will help acquaint you with JavaScript's breakneck speed.

Expo

Recently the React Native team has partnered with Expo (*https://expo.io*) to deliver React Native applications in development without running a local development environment. This is a great way to explore React Native and get a taste, but you will likely want to work with the hardware at some point, at which point a local development environment will be critical to your productivity.

1.1 Setting Up Your Development Environment

If you're working with any of these tools in other web projects, you might find yourself having to troubleshoot your environment. Like a carpenter arriving on a job site, you need to know how all the tools work and if they need to be fixed.

React Native is a package that includes three programming environments: Node.js, iOS, and Android. NPM, the Node Package Manager, needs to be in good working order.

Problem

React Native is a software library that depends on a lot of different tools. How do we know if all of them are configured correctly? Let's review them and make sure.

Node and Watchman

Node.js (usually abbreviated to "Node") enables your computer to run JavaScript locally in the same way that a web browser runs JavaScript when a web page is executed. Because Node.js runs directly on top of your operating system, Node code can wrap or bind to C libraries and solve the same programming problems that are suited to languages like PHP, Python, PERL, and Ruby.

Watchman is a little utility that watches for file changes locally and triggers events. This tool makes it possible to execute updated code on your Simulator without having to recompile the whole project. Installation is quick and easy (*http://bit.ly/ 2FUNzyJ*).

Installing Node.js

Installing Node depends on your operating system. The best place to get started is The Node.js website (*https://nodejs.org*). If you are running on Mac OS, you may find it preferable to install Node.js through Homebrew, a Mac OS package manager.

Check that Node is properly installed. You may find yourself with many versions of Node.js installed on your computer. Version managers like the Node Version Manager (NVM) (*https://github.com/creationix/nvm*) can help you keep different versions of Node installed, with each development project configured with its own version of Node.

POSIX-style operating systems (Linux, BSD, Mac OS) can rely on symbolic links (symlink) to support multiple versions.

You shouldn't be surprised if you have two versions of Node installed using Homebrew with Mac OS. This is what your installation should look like, except with your own username and date information next to the directories listed:

```
$> which node
/usr/local/bin/node
$> node -v
v8.6.0
```

I'm using version 8.6.0 of Node; however, if I check the Homebrew directory (default is */usr/local/Cellar*) I will discover a symlink (alias to the actual location):

```
$>ls -l /usr/local/bin/node
lrwxr-xr-x  1 jon  admin  29 27 Sep 15:14 /usr/local/bin/node ->
../Cellar/node/8.6.0/bin/node
```

A little more digging and I'll find other versions of Node that have been superseded:

```
$>ls -l /usr/local/Cellar/node
 total 0
 drwxr-xr-x  14 jon  admin  476 11 May 14:14 7.10.0
 drwxr-xr-x  14 jon  admin  476 25 Apr 13:41 7.9.0
 drwxr-xr-x  14 jon  admin  448 27 Sep 15:14 8.6.0
```

Your results will likely be different; however, what is important is that you have a recent version of Node installed and accessible to your project.

NPM

The NPM is two things: a package management tool running from the command line and a global catalog of open source packages available at your fingertips.

The `react-native` package in NPM includes JavaScript ES6 modules that rely on platform-specific code. For example, the `<Text />` React Native component is implemented by *RCTText.m* in iOS and *ReactTextView.java* in Android.

What About Using Yarn?

React Native has historically been set up with NPM, but Yarn is gaining ground in the JavaScript community. Yarn is a faster alternative to NPM that still relies on the NPM registry. A *yarn.lock* file ensures that dependencies are maintained correctly. Yarn will start by checking the *yarn.lock* file, then look for *package.json*, making the transition to Yarn seamless.

NPM packages can live globally or within a *node_modules* folder for a given project. React Native is best installed globally, whereas project-related dependencies should be downloaded to a local folder. This approach allows you to run React Native's command-line tool, `react-native-cli`, anywhere. Specific versions of the React Native can be part of your project's dependencies.

Check that NPM is properly installed

```
$> which npm
/usr/local/bin/npm
```

Your terminal should return with a path. Check the version:

```
$> npm -v
4.2.0
```

Install the React Native command-line tools

```
$> npm install -g react-native-cli
```

Xcode (required for iOS)

Xcode is Apple's official development environment for building and running applications on Mac OS and iOS. You will need Xcode (available only on Mac OS) installed in order to compile the React Native components that are backed by Objective-C and Swift.

Xcode also ships with command-line tools, which are necessary to build code from the command line and to bind to the Mac OS libraries from Node.js.

Running Xcode Beta

With regular updates to iOS, you may have a beta of Xcode on your development machine. Having multiple versions of Xcode will result in multiple versions of the iOS Simulator. I've found it best under these circumstances to launch the Simulator from Xcode rather than the command line.

JDK

Android and Java go together like sugar and butter—together they make delicious experiences possible. React Native on Android is no different. The React components you write in JavaScript will ultimately touch the Android Java Virtual Machine. In order to run Android locally, you need the Java Development Kit (JDK) installed.

Download the JDK (minimum version 8) from the Oracle website (*http://bit.ly/ 1X9h0Ea*).

Android Studio

Android Studio is the official development environment for building and deploying Android applications. It's free to download (*http://bit.ly/2Dbnmeu*). Once you have it set up, it comes with yet another package manager. Fortunately, the React Native Getting Started guide goes through all the details step by step (*http://bit.ly/2GWQDfo*).

1.2 Writing ES6 with Babel

Babel brings a 20-year programming language into the twenty-first century. With Babel, you can write JavaScript with some syntactic enhancements that make your code more expressive. Common patterns, like transforming data structures, handling this in the appropriate scope, and inheriting from classes become part of the native development experience.

Babel enables these syntactic improvements to the language through a series of *syntax transformers*. Each transformer runs through your code, taking newer ES6 language features and transforming them into equivalent behaviors in JavaScript syntax.

The following ES6 code is transformed automatically using the `react-native` preset.

Save the following to a file called *babel-transform.js*:

```
AsyncStorage.getItem("loginParameters").then( (login) => {
        this.setState({ login });
});
```

From the command line, run:

```
$> babel babel-transform.js
```

Babel should return (formatted for readability):

```
var _this=this;

AsyncStorage.getItem("loginParams").then( function(login) {
        _this.setState({
                login: login
        });
});
```

The React Native preset has:

1. Expanded { `login` } into { `login: login` }.
2. Replaced the `=>` operator with a reference to `_this` defined in the outer method scope.

Working with React Native almost always means using React and the JSX preprocessor. The JSX preprocessor enables XML syntax inside of JavaScript files. The Babel transpiler has plug-ins for handling JSX out of the box.

Any of the React Native initialization scripts will include a *.babelrc* file in the root folder of the application. It should look like this:

```
{
  "presets": ["react-native"]
}
```

At the time of this writing, the React Native preset is shorthand for the following Babel transpilations:

- `class-properties`
- `es2015-arrow-functions`
- `es2015-block-scoping`
- `es2015-classes`

- es2015-computed-properties
- es2015-destructuring
- es2015-for-of
- es2015-function-name
- es2015-literals
- es2015-modules-commonjs
- es2015-parameters
- es2015-shorthand-properties
- es2015-spread
- es2015-template-literals
- flow-strip-types
- object-assign
- object-rest-spread
- react-display-name
- react-jsx-source
- react-jsx

Problem

In the previous example, es2015-shorthand-properties and es2015-arrow-functions were applied to the one-line code snippet referenced at the beginning of this recipe.

Let's add a new syntax transformer that will add support for do blocks to our environment.

Solution

The do block is a helpful combination of a switch operator and a function. You may find this syntax useful when switching out the appropriate React component based on something in this.state or this.props:

```
$>npm i  --save-dev babel-plugin-transform-do-expressions
```

Create a simple file called *babel.js* in your project folder:

```
WelcomeHeader = (username) => do {
  if(username !== undefined) {
    `Welcome, ${username}.`;
  } else {
```

```
      'Hello there, stranger!';
    }
}

console.log(WelcomeHeader('Mr. Robot'));
console.log(WelcomeHeader());
```

Add the transform to *babel.rc*:

```
{
  "presets": ["react-native"],
  "plugins": ["syntax-do-expressions"]
}
```

Now try converting the file with Babel:

```
$>babel babel.js
WelcomeHeader=function WelcomeHeader(username)
{return username!==undefined?'Welcome,
'+username+'.':'Hello there, stranger!';};
console.log(WelcomeHeader('Mr. Robot'));
console.log(WelcomeHeader());
```

Try running the code example with babel-node (*https://babeljs.io/docs/usage/cli/*):

```
$>babel-node babel.js
Welcome, Mr. Robot.
Hello there, stranger!
```

See Also

Support for decorators is upcoming in Babel. Currently this transform can be handled using the transform-decorators-legacy (*http://bit.ly/2GX9kPW*) transform.

Decorators are functions that wrap existing code. Since *higher order functions—func-*tions that call JSX components in other functions—are wrapping code, the *decorator transform* provides syntax for declaring this wrapping code.

1.3 Organizing Project Files

Organizing code is tricky. One of the greatest software engineers of our time, Robert C. Martin, shared the following insight about directory structures and how they impact software architecture:

> So what does the architecture of your application scream? ... do they scream: Rails, or Spring/Hibernate, or ASP? ... Tell readers about the system, not about the frameworks you used in your system. If you are building a health-care system, then when new programmers look at the source repository, their first impression should be: "Oh, this is a health-care system."

> —Robert C. Martin, *Screaming Architecture* (30 September 2011)

With tools like `react-native init` and `create-react-native-app` we're given a great starting point for structuring our application. You should treat this as a starting point and nothing more.

Create React Native App

If you are looking for some project scaffolding, the React Community has put together `create-react-native-app` (*http://bit.ly/2nQF0Oi*), a library that will help you set up a React Native project with some helpful defaults. This is a great tool as long as your project is purely written in JavaScript and a limited list of supported Expo libraries. Eventually, you may want to *eject* the app from the scaffolding and manage the build process yourself.

Problem

Your React Native application is taking off! You can barely keep the bits on the digital shelves. You are responding to feature requests as soon as they come in. The result is lots of new code. The architectural seams of your project are giving way: code is being duplicated and you find yourself repeating components and business logic. Worst of all, these duplicates are hard to find because your project structure doesn't surface dependencies to your project team.

Solution

There's no one-size-fits-all solution to how to structure your application. Most React Native applications will have directories that describe *components*, *screens*, *state management*, and *utilities*. You will know that your structure fits well when you strike a balance: having directories with a cluster of files that implement a feature and not having too many folders to keep track of at any given time.

Some examples

It's helpful to see the end in the beginning: how sophisticated will the application ultimately become? Will it need to be localized into multiple languages? Will it have to support different user types or roles? Following are three example folder structures from some popular open source React Native applications.

Notice how they all communicate a blueprint of the main aspects of the application.

Bullet

Bullet is a cryptocurrency management tool:

```
.
├── actions
├── api
```

```
├── assets
│   ├── fonts
│   └── icons
├── components
│   ├── adverts
│   ├── bull
│   ├── converter
│   ├── currencies
│   ├── errors
│   ├── graphs
│   ├── navigations
│   ├── news
│   ├── portfolio
│   ├── search
│   └── utilities
├── configuration
├── constants
├── middleware
├── mock
├── navigations
├── properties
│   ├── languages
│   └── themes
├── reducers
├── schematics
├── screens
├── styles
└── utilities
```

Chain Conference app

This mobile application was built for a conference:

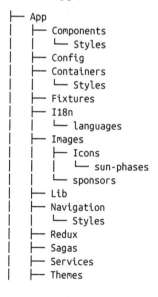

```
├── App
│   ├── Components
│   │   └── Styles
│   ├── Config
│   ├── Containers
│   │   └── Styles
│   ├── Fixtures
│   ├── I18n
│   │   └── languages
│   ├── Images
│   │   ├── Icons
│   │   │   └── sun-phases
│   │   └── sponsors
│   ├── Lib
│   ├── Navigation
│   │   └── Styles
│   ├── Redux
│   ├── Sagas
│   ├── Services
│   ├── Themes
```

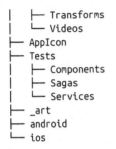

```
|      ├── Transforms
|      └── Videos
├── AppIcon
├── Tests
|      ├── Components
|      ├── Sagas
|      └── Services
├── _art
├── android
└── ios
```

MatterMost mobile chat application

A sophisticated asynchronous chat application frontend to a cloud-based team collaboration product:

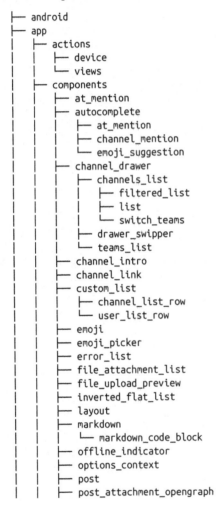

```
├── android
├── app
|   ├── actions
|   |   ├── device
|   |   └── views
|   ├── components
|   |   ├── at_mention
|   |   ├── autocomplete
|   |   |   ├── at_mention
|   |   |   ├── channel_mention
|   |   |   └── emoji_suggestion
|   |   ├── channel_drawer
|   |   |   ├── channels_list
|   |   |   |   ├── filtered_list
|   |   |   |   ├── list
|   |   |   |   └── switch_teams
|   |   |   ├── drawer_swipper
|   |   |   └── teams_list
|   |   ├── channel_intro
|   |   ├── channel_link
|   |   ├── custom_list
|   |   |   ├── channel_list_row
|   |   |   └── user_list_row
|   |   ├── emoji
|   |   ├── emoji_picker
|   |   ├── error_list
|   |   ├── file_attachment_list
|   |   ├── file_upload_preview
|   |   ├── inverted_flat_list
|   |   ├── layout
|   |   ├── markdown
|   |   |   └── markdown_code_block
|   |   ├── offline_indicator
|   |   ├── options_context
|   |   ├── post
|   |   ├── post_attachment_opengraph
```

```
│   │   ├── post_body
│   │   ├── post_body_additional_content
│   │   ├── post_header
│   │   ├── post_list
│   │   ├── post_profile_picture
│   │   ├── post_textbox
│   │   │   └── components
│   │   │       └── typing
│   │   ├── profile_picture
│   │   ├── radio_button
│   │   ├── reactions
│   │   ├── root
│   │   ├── search_bar
│   │   ├── search_preview
│   │   ├── slack_attachments
│   │   ├── status_bar
│   │   └── status_icons
│   ├── constants
│   ├── i18n
│   ├── mattermost_managed
│   ├── notification_preferences
│   ├── push_notifications
│   ├── reducers
│   │   ├── device
│   │   ├── navigation
│   │   └── views
│   ├── screens
│   │   ├── about
│   │   ├── add_reaction
│   │   ├── channel
│   │   │   └── channel_post_list
│   │   ├── channel_add_members
│   │   ├── channel_info
│   │   ├── channel_members
│   │   ├── code
│   │   ├── create_channel
│   │   ├── edit_post
│   │   ├── image_preview
│   │   ├── load_team
│   │   ├── login
│   │   ├── login_options
│   │   ├── mfa
│   │   ├── more_channels
│   │   ├── more_dms
│   │   │   └── selected_users
│   │   ├── notification
│   │   ├── options_modal
│   │   ├── root
│   │   ├── search
│   │   ├── select_server
│   │   ├── select_team
│   │   ├── settings
```

```
│   │   │   ├── advanced_settings
│   │   │   ├── general
│   │   │   ├── notification_settings
│   │   │   ├── notification_settings_email
│   │   │   ├── notification_settings_mentions
│   │   │   ├── notification_settings_mentions_keywords
│   │   │   ├── notification_settings_mobile
│   │   │   └── settings_item
│   │   ├── sso
│   │   ├── thread
│   │   └── user_profile
│   ├── selectors
│   ├── store
│   ├── styles
│   └── utils
│       └── sentry
├── assets
├── fastlane
└── test
```

Components

React Native applications will use React components. Each React component will live in its own file. These components are usually *presentational components*,[1] meaning that they can be used without any knowledge of an external dependency. React applications assume that it is the component's responsibility to declare what it needs from its consumer. A simple component could just be a single JavaScript file in the *components/* folder.

Here are some files you may wish to include with a component. This is an example of a Dropdown component that depends on a few different files:

JSX component file
    components/dropdown/dropdown.js

Specific styles
    components/dropdown/styles.js

Subcomponents
    components/dropdown/row.js

Index file
    components/dropdown/index.js

---

1 Dan Abramov discusses the difference between presentational components and container components in greater detail in this Medium post (*http://bit.ly/2Er6xAc*).

Writing Cross-Platform Components

Sometimes the iOS and Android version of a component differ so greatly that it makes sense to have a completely different component for each. The React Native compiler is intelligent enough to infer the correct variation based on the file suffix and folder structure. For example, a `Dropdown` component can be inside of a */dropdown* folder with three files: *dropdown.android.js*, *dropdown.ios.js*, and *index.js*. The *index.js* will automatically reference the correct version of the component based on the suffix:

```
import Dropdown from './dropdown';
export default Dropdown;
```

The rest of your application is spared from having to know that there are two implementations of `Dropdown`!

Screens

Screens, also called *containers*, are components that also have some sort of state management. Most applications will have some library or framework for handling state across different pages. By using a library like `React Navigation` described in Recipe 2.4, you will already be indicating which components are screens that a user will navigate to. Not all containers can be considered screens; for example, a login form could be considered a container that will rest inside a number of different screens.

```
// components/root/container.js
import Guest from "../guest";
import LoggedIn from "../loggedIn";
import { StackNavigator } from 'react-navigation';

const RouteConfig = {
  guest: { screen: Guest.container },
  loggedIn: { screen: LoggedIn.container },
}
export default StackNavigator(RouteConfig);
```

Screens are often kept in their own folder, making the state management dependencies very clear.

GraphQL mutations
    `components/guest/mutations.js`

GraphQL queries
    `components/guest/queries.js`

Redux actions
    `components/guest/actions.js`

Redux types
    `components/guest/types.js`

State management

Global state management is often handled outside the *components/* and *screens/* directories.

GraphQL libraries like Relay and Apollo will bring their own conventions for managing GraphQL queries and mutations. If you decide to use a Flux-inspired architecture, like Redux or MobX, it may make sense to keep *Action Creators* or any code that the screen may call to talk to the larger application in the folder. See Recipe 2.5 for an example of global state management.

Utilities

Most projects will also include files with functions, business logic, or other helper code. These files will often live in a *lib/* or *utils/* folder. If you find yourself writing a lot of utility code, it may be a sign that a separate package or module needs to be written that can simply be referenced by your React Native application.

Discussion

Let the application domain dictate the structure. For example, you may be working on a reporting application with hundreds of little components that come together in a beautiful mobile dashboard. You will likely have hundreds of components in a */components* folder with slight variations.

Another application might be dozens of little forms as part of a customer loan application. In this case state might need to be managed across views and validated throughout. Business logic might find its way peppered through the components or in some state management library like *redux*. Another approach is called Ducks (*http://bit.ly/2BeMEdr*), a proposed way of structuring redux-driven applications.

How do you know if your project files are well organized? Interview someone on your team and see if they can find their way around the the project intuitively. If you find yourself changing files across several directories every time a new, distinct feature is developed, then you might want to consider reorganizing your project files.

1.4 Dealing with Catastrophic Failure

Like a mousse that won't set, sometimes we have to face catastrophic failure. Fortunately React Native provides a set of common tools for debugging applications.

Problem

You have an error and you don't know what you changed or you find yourself with a warning and are struggling to track it down.

Solution

Unlike real cooking, we can save ourselves the unpleasant task of starting from scratch simply by using version control. Even if I don't plan on sharing my React Native experiments with the world, I make a point of using `git` locally to keep different versions of my project. This way I can refactor away and always have a waypoint in my development trail to refer to. A `git checkout` is all that's required to undo a fatal red screen of death as shown in Figure 1-1.

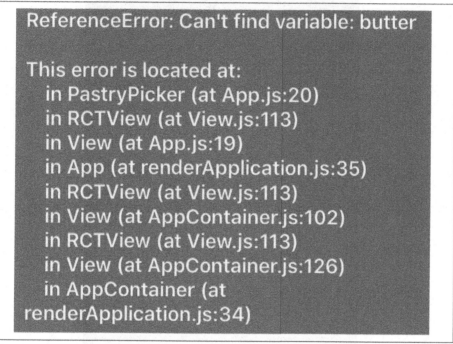

Figure 1-1. The React Native red screen of death (RedBox)

Rely on the React Native debugger. You can access it by doing a `Hardware > Shake Gesture` in the iOS Simulator. With Android, you will need to run ⌘M on a Mac. You can refresh your app by typing `rr` in the Android Simulator or ⌘R in the iOS Simulator. See more details in the React Native Debugging Guide (*http://bit.ly/2EJxlZX*). See an example of the React Native debugging toolbar on iOS in Figure 1-2.

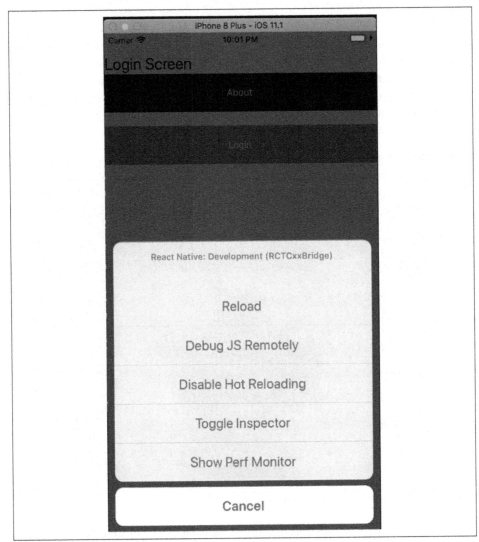

Figure 1-2. React Native applications have a debugging toolbar

Because React Native relies on JavaScript, you can use console.log() or the debug
ger directive in your components to output a variable or stop the render midstream
and treat the Chrome console as an expression viewer.

If you think everything should be running correctly, try quitting the React Native
Packager (usually a node process), clean your build with Xcode or Android Studio,
and reinstall and run the application.

If your application uses the popular *Redux* state management library, the `redux-devtools-extension` (*http://bit.ly/2nQfit0*) might help with stepping through the state changes in your application. You might also want to try the `react-devtools` standalone debugger (*http://bit.ly/2nvFKar*) provided by Facebook. The React Native Debugging guide (*http://bit.ly/2EpxvrD*) provides some helpful insights as well. Lastly, Reactotron (*https://github.com/infinitered/reactotron*) provides a desktop application for inspecting React Native applications in real time.

Discussion

There are a number of developer tools for React. If something works with React, there's a good chance that someone is making it work with React Native.

CHAPTER 2

Living in the React Native Ecosystem

The smallest logical unit in a React application is the component: a function that transforms input into a nested set of views rendered based on a set of parameters. The React ecosystem is overflowing with these components; oftentimes we import them from external libraries.

This chapter will introduce you to the mechanics involved in importing components, building your own components, and using JavaScript libraries that support the React approach to building complex applications.

2.1 Stop Repeating Yourself: Implement Custom Components

React applications with lots of components that do one thing are easier to compose, organize, and maintain.

Problem

Your application has a `<Header />` on every screen. With over a dozen screens, how do you avoid writing a haiku of configuration every time you build a new part of the application?

Solution

Cut down the repetition by implementing your own `<ScreenHeader />` component.

In this example, I'm using the `react-native-elements` component library to render a `<Header />` component. See Recipe 2.3 for an example of how to import a custom component.

Global Styles

You will notice in this example the references to `colors` and `global`
`Styles`. These were imported from an external file at the top of the
file: `import { colors, globalStyles } from '../styles';`.

See Chapter 3 for more details on defining global colors and styles.

A *Home* screen has the following JSX inside the `render()` function:

```
<View style={globalStyles.headerContainer}>
  <Header
    leftComponent={
      <Button
        icon={{name: 'arrow-back'}}
        buttonStyle={{
          backgroundColor: null,
          padding: 0,
        }}
        title=''
        color={colors.WHITE}
        onPress={this.backPressed}
      />}
    centerComponent={
      <Text
        style={globalStyles.siteHeaderText}
      >{this.props.data.me.first_name}</Text>
    }
    rightComponent={
      <Button
        icon={{name: 'home'}}
        buttonStyle={{
          backgroundColor: null,
          padding: 0,
        }}
        title=''
        color={colors.WHITE}
        onPress={this.goHome}
      />}
  />
</View>
```

A *Course* screen has something that looks very similar:

```
<View style={globalStyles.headerContainer}>
  <Header
    leftComponent={
      <Button
        icon={{name: 'arrow-back'}}
        buttonStyle={{
          backgroundColor: null,
          padding: 0,
        }}
```

```
        title=''
        color={colors.WHITE}
        onPress={this.back}
      />}
    centerComponent={
      <Text
        style={globalStyles.siteHeaderText}
      >{this.course().name}</Text>
    }
    rightComponent={
      <Button
        icon={{name: 'settings'}}
        buttonStyle={{
          backgroundColor: null,
          padding: 0,
        }}
        title=''
        color={colors.WHITE}
        onPress={this.goHome}
      />}
  />
</View>
```

I see a lot of repetition, especially given that every single screen will have some variation of this `<Header />`. Ideally, I would be able to reference a component that emphasizes the differences and hides the complexity:

```
<ScreenHeader
  leftComponentIcon='arrow-back'
  leftOnPress={this.back}
  centerText={this.course().name}
  rightIcon='settings'
  rightOnPress{this.goHome}
  />
```

Create a new file in your project in a *components* folder—*components/screenHeader.js*:

```
import React, { Component } from 'react';

import {
  Text,
  View,
} from 'react-native';

import {
  Button,
  Header,
} from 'react-native-elements';

import { colors, globalStyles } from '../styles';

import PropTypes from 'prop-types';
```

```
class ScreenHeader extends Component {

  render() {
    return <View style={globalStyles.headerContainer}>
      <Header
      leftComponent={{
        <Button
          icon={{name: this.props.leftIcon}}
          buttonStyle={{
            backgroundColor: null,
            padding: 0,
          }}
          title=''
          color={colors.WHITE}
          onPress={this.props.leftOnPress}
        />
      }
      centerComponent={{
        <Text style={globalStyles.siteHeaderText}>{this.props.centerText}</Text>
      }
      rightComponent={{
        <Button
          icon={{name: this.props.rightIcon}}
          buttonStyle={{
            backgroundColor: null,
            padding: 0,
          }}
          title=''
          color={colors.WHITE}
          onPress={this.props.rightOnPress}
        />}
      />
    </View>
  }
}
ScreenHeader.propTypes = {
  leftIcon: PropTypes.string,
  rightIcon: PropTypes.string,
  centerText: PropTypes.string,
  leftOnPress: PropTypes.func,
  rightOnPress: PropTypes.func,
};
export default ScreenHeader;
```

We can now keep our screen code focused on the different implementations and expose an API with a handful of PropTypes that the developer can pass to <Screen Header />.

2.2 Adding an Open Source Progress Bar

Almost all applications rely on activities that require the user to wait for an operation to complete. In some cases this can simply be the time required for a client to receive a message from a web server or third-party API. Another example might be waiting for an image to be processed in a background thread on the device.

Problem

How do we communicate to users that they need to wait?

Solution

Let's add a progress bar. This is a great task to introduce the steps required to import React Native components. Here we will import the component and discuss linking the libART.a library to our project. In Recipe 3.4 we will create an indeterminate progress animation.

Most open source React Native components have comprehensive *README.md* files that describe how to include the component and whether it's been designed to work in iOS, Android, or both.

Discussion

 Make sure the development server isn't running when you add new packages using Yarn or Node. The React Packager may not pick up the new libraries and you will probably need to run react-native link and rebuild the project binary.

Start by adding react-native-progress to your project:

```
$> npm install react-native-progress --save
$> react-native link
```

Usually calling react-native link is all that's required to add the necessary iOS or Android libraries to the project build process. In this case, react-native-progress relies on a special library for iOS called *ReactART* for drawing pie charts.

Let's link the ReactART library manually after calling react-native link. Figure 2-1 shows a project I created called RNScratchPad in Xcode.

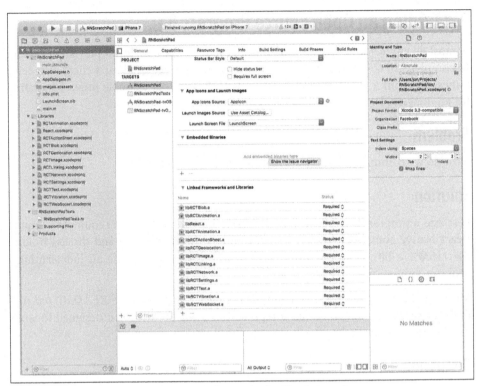

Figure 2-1. The RNScratchPad project shown in the Xcode interface

Expand the *Libraries* folder in the project view, as shown in Figure 2-2.

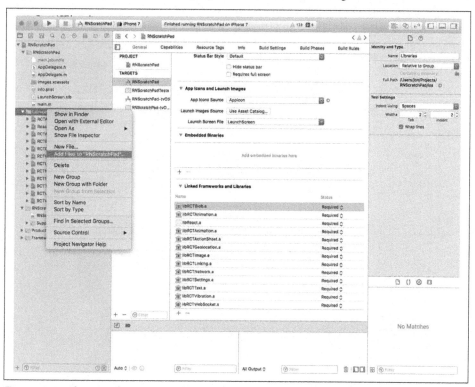

Figure 2-2. Choose Libraries → Add Files to add a new reference under Libraries

Start by adding a reference to the *ART.xcodeproject* file included with React Native in *node_modules/react-native/Libraries/ART* (Figure 2-3).

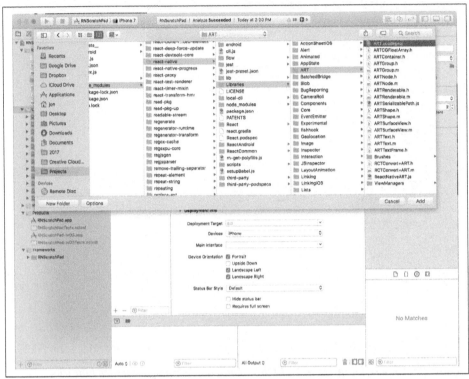

Figure 2-3. Find ART.xcodeproject in the react-native project files

Under Linked Frameworks and Libraries, find the + symbol. libART.a should be available as a library to add to your project (Figure 2-4).

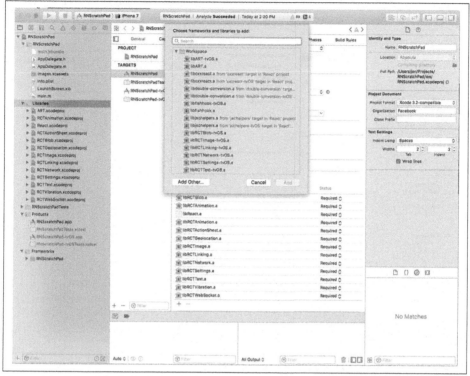

Figure 2-4. Select libART.a from the list

Your project configuration should now include this reference (Figure 2-5).

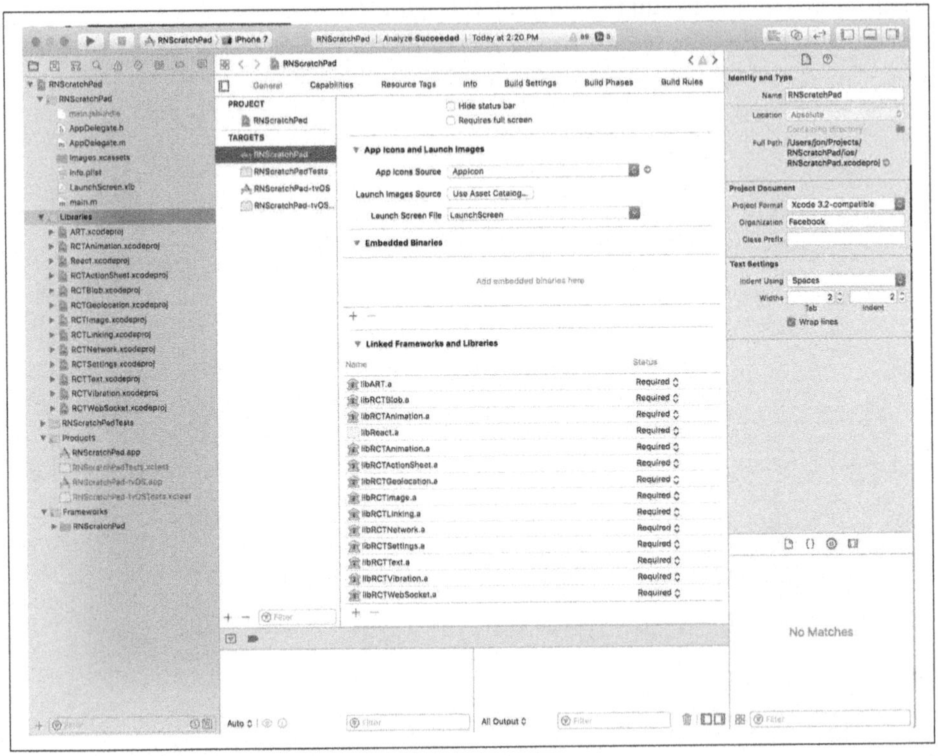

Figure 2-5. Reference the project in your configuration

Now rebuild the project and deploy the app on your Simulator or development device. Let's add a simple progress bar to one of our components:

```
import React, { Component } from 'react';
import {
  View
} from 'react-native';

import * as Progress from 'react-native-progress';

export default class App extends Component<{}> {
  render() {
    return (
      <View style={{flex: 1, justifyContent: 'center', alignItems: 'center' }}>
        <Progress.Pie progress={0.2} size={50} color="#2245FF" />
      </View>
    );
  }
}
```

You should see something like this in the Simulator:

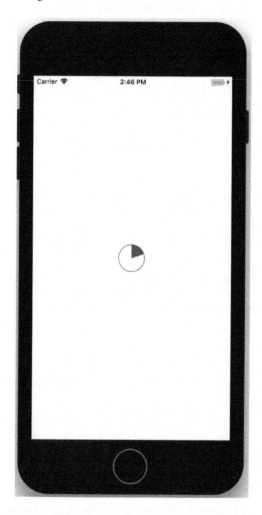

Notice that by changing the progress attribute, the progress bar changes.

We can animate progress changes by relying on a local this.state.progress variable. Here is a more complete example:

```
import React, { Component } from 'react';
import {
  Text,
  TouchableHighlight,
  View
} from 'react-native';

import * as Progress from 'react-native-progress';
```

```
export default class App extends Component<{}> {
  constructor(props) {
    super(props);
    this.state = { progress: 0.2 }
  }

  randomProgress = () => {
    const progress = Math.random();
    this.setState({ progress });
  }

  render() {
    return (
      <View style={{flex: 1, justifyContent: 'center', alignItems: 'center' }}>
        <View style={{marginBottom: 10}}>
          <Progress.Pie borderWidth={2} borderColor='#62321B'
          unfilledColor='#F5F5F5'
            progress={this.state.progress} size={100} color='#D6C598' />
        </View>
        <TouchableHighlight onPress={this.randomProgress}
          style={{padding: 10, backgroundColor: '#CACACA', borderRadius: 5 }}>
          <Text style={{fontSize: 18, fontWeight: 'bold' }} >Apple Pie Me!</Text>
        </TouchableHighlight>
      </View>
    );
  }
}
```

Tapping <TouchableHighlight /> will result in different pie servings!

See Also

Learn how to animate the progress bar in Recipe 3.4.

2.3 Sharing Custom Components

You have a collection of components that are worth using on multiple projects. Copying and pasting them between projects is not going to cut it.

Problem

How do you reuse a whole section of your React Native application in another project? For example, you might have created a component library that includes all of the visual identity requirements for your product. Naturally, you want to share this across multiple projects and only have to make visual changes for these components in one place. This approach enables reuse and also means that you can version portions of your application more easily and reinforce your product's architectural boundaries. In my case, I've built a <PastryPicker /> component—critical to visualizing the relative amount of flour, sugar, butter, and eggs across baked goods (Figure 2-6).

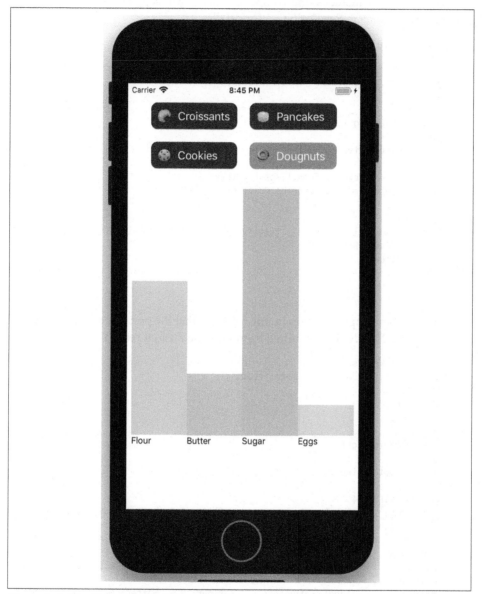

Figure 2-6. The PastryPicker Component

Solution

The sample project includes one component that I will separate into its own NPM package, *pastryPicker.js*. See Recipe 1.1 for details.

The main application, *App.js*, references `<PastryPicker />`:

```
// App.js
import React, { Component } from 'react';
import {
  Text,
  TouchableHighlight,
  View
} from 'react-native';

import { PastryPicker } from './pastryPicker';
export default class App extends Component {
  render() {
    return (
        <View style={{flex: 1, justifyContent: 'center', alignItems: 'center' }}>
          <PastryPicker />
        </View>
    );
  }
};
```

The *PastryPicker* component lives in one file (note that the pastry icon characters pictured in Figure 2-6 have been omitted from the code for font reasons):

```
// pastryPicker.js
import React, { Component } from 'react';
import {
  Animated,
  StyleSheet,
  Text,
  TouchableHighlight,
  View,
} from 'react-native';

const PASTRIES = {
  croissant:    { label: 'Croissants',   flour: 0.7, butter: 0.5, sugar: 0.2,
  eggs: 0 },
  cookie:       { label: 'Cookies',      flour: 0.5, butter: 0.4, sugar: 0.5,
  eggs: 0.2},
  pancake:      { label: 'Pancakes',     flour: 0.7, butter: 0.5, sugar: 0.3,
  eggs: 0.3 },
  doughnut:     { label: 'Dougnuts',     flour: 0.5, butter: 0.2, sugar: 0.8,
  eggs: 0.1 },
};

export default class PastryPicker extends Component {
  constructor(props) {
    super(props);
```

```
      this.state = {
        selectedPastry: 'croissant'
      }
    }

    setPastry = (selectedPastry) => {
      this.setState({ selectedPastry });
    }

    renderIngredient(backgroundColor, flex, label) {
      return <View  style={styles.ingredientColumn}>
        <View style={styles.bar} />
        <View style={{ backgroundColor, flex }} />
        <View style={styles.label}><Text>{label}</Text></View>
      </View>
    }

    render() {
      const { flour, butter, sugar, eggs } = PASTRIES[this.state.selectedPastry];
      return <View style={styles.pastryPicker}>
          <View style={styles.buttons}>
            {
              Object.keys(PASTRIES).map( (key) => <View key={key}
              style={styles.buttonContainer}>
                <TouchableHighlight
                  style={[styles.button, {
                    backgroundColor: key === this.state.selectedPastry ?
                    '#CD7734' : '#54250B' }
                  ]} underlayColor='CD7734' onPress={() => {
                  this.setPastry(key) } }>
                    <Text style={styles.buttonText} >{PASTRIES[key].label}</Text>
                </TouchableHighlight>
              </View>)
            }
          </View>
        <View style={styles.ingredientContainer}>
          {this.renderIngredient('#F2D8A6', flour, 'Flour')}
          {this.renderIngredient('#FFC049', butter, 'Butter')}
          {this.renderIngredient('#CACACA', sugar, 'Sugar')}
          {this.renderIngredient('#FFDE59', eggs, 'Eggs')}
        </View>
      </View>
    }
  }

const styles = StyleSheet.create({
  pastryPicker: {
    flex: 1,
    flexDirection: 'column',
    margin: 20,
  },
  ingredientContainer: {
```

```
    flex: 1,
    flexDirection: 'row',
  },
  ingredientColumn: {
    flexDirection: 'column',
    flex: 1,
    justifyContent: 'flex-end',
  },
  buttonContainer: {
    margin: 10,
  },
  bar: {
    alignSelf: 'flex-start',
    flexGrow: 0,
  },
  button: {
    padding: 10,
    minWidth: 140,
    justifyContent: 'center',
    backgroundColor: '#5A8282',
    borderRadius: 10,
  },
  buttonText: {
    fontSize: 18,
    color: '#FFF',
  },
  buttons: {
    flexDirection: 'column',
    flexWrap: 'wrap',
    paddingRight: 20,
    paddingLeft: 20,
    flex: 0.3,
  },
  label: {
    flex: 0.2,
  },
});
```

Discussion

Let's go through the steps required to pull a collection of components into a separate project where they can be included in multiple React Native projects.

In Recipe 2.2 we referenced an external NPM package for rendering progress bars. Our component is much simpler: it relies entirely on existing React Native components, which means that in our case we can simply create an NPM package with the correct dependencies.

Assuming you have NPM correctly installed, you should be able to create a new package from the command line. Create a folder for the package and run npm init inside it:

```
$> mkdir react-native-pastry-picker
$> cd react-native-pastry-picker
$> npm init
This utility will walk you through creating a package.json file.
It only covers the most common items, and tries to guess sensible defaults.

See `npm help json` for definitive documentation on these fields
and exactly what they do.

Use `npm install <pkg>` afterwards to install a package and
save it as a dependency in the package.json file.

package name: (projects) react-native-pastry-picker
...
```

You will be presented with a series of questions (package name, version, main entry point, etc.). Use the defaults for now; you can change them later. Only the package name is important since that will be the package folder and the reference for the main application.

 An emerging convention in the React Native community is to prefix component libraries with react-native- and host them on GitHub.

If the command is successful, a *package.json* file should be automatically created. Let's add React as a *development dependency*—a required package for development purposes:

```
$> npm i --save-dev react
```

You should now have a *node_modules* folder and a *package.lock* file in the project file. Your *package.json* file should look something like this:

```
{
  "name": "react-native-pastry-picker",
  "version": "1.0.0",
  "description": "",
  "main": "index.js",
  "scripts": {
    "test": "echo \"Error: no test specified\" && exit 1"
  },
  "author": "Jon Lebensold",
  "license": "MIT",
  "devDependencies": {
    "react": "^16.0.0"
  }
}
```

You will notice that key `main` points to *index.js*. The *index.js* file should serve as a manifest for all public components. Let's do a sanity check of our component by creating an *index.js* file that wraps a simple `<Text />` component:

```
import React, { Component } from 'react';
import {
  Text,
  View,
} from 'react-native';

export class SanityCheck extends Component {
  render() {
    return <View><Text>I am an externally referenced component!</Text></View>
  }
}
```

We can now add the component to our main project with a relative reference and restart our development server. Once the package is ready to be published, we can change our *package.json* file to reference the published name on *npmjs.com*.

```
$> npm install --save ../react-native-pastry-picker
$> yarn start --reset-cache
```

Dependency Management

Referencing packages locally from *package.json* sometimes causes the React Native Packager to forget to refresh the internal cache. I recommend using Yarn instead of NPM or `react-native start` when relying on a locally referenced dependency.

Learn how to install Yarn at *https://yarnpkg.com/en/docs/install*.

We can adjust our *App.js* file to reference the new dependency:

```
import React, { Component } from 'react';
import {
  View
} from 'react-native';
import { SanityCheck } from 'react-native-pastry-picker'
export default class App extends Component<{}> {
  render() {
    return (
        <View style={{flex: 1, justifyContent: 'center',
        alignItems: 'center' }}>
          <SanityCheck />
      </View>
    );
  }
}
```

The main application should render <SanityCheck /> as though it was part of the local library. You can now safely move the components out of the main project and update the *index.js* in react-native-pastry-picker to reference the components internally like this:

```
export { default as PastryPicker } from './pastryPicker';
```

See Also

Once your component library is taking shape, make sure you update the *package.json* file with the appropriate metadata fields. You will probably want to publish the project to NPM (*http://bit.ly/2nTlvVo*) so that it can be referenced like any other React Native package.

If you need to call native libraries, then more setup will be required. I recommend looking at well-supported packages like react-native-camera (*http://bit.ly/2C2DM7s*). Remember that you can use this same approach for sharing application constants, stylesheets, and default typography or image assets as well!

2.4 Routing Between Login Screens

Most mobile applications need to provide a mechanism for someone to travel between screens seamlessly. The classic example is a list of items, where tapping any item allows the user to drill into the list element. It's also often the case that there is a portion of the application that is available to someone logged in.

Problem

How do we maintain all these different screens without losing track of the global state of our application? How do we ensure seamless transitions between pages? The React Navigation community project (*https://reactnavigation.org/*) aims to address these challenges by providing a set of nesting *navigator* components.

Solution

Start by adding react-navigation to your project:

```
$> npm install --save react-navigation
```

Let's break out our application into three navigators:

Root navigator
    The top-level navigator for the application.

Guest navigator
    Provides screen navigation before a user is logged in.

User navigator

Provides screen navigation inside the application. The root navigator is passed by reference via screenProps.

See how the navigators deliver the Login, About, Profile, and Dashboard screens in Figure 2-7.

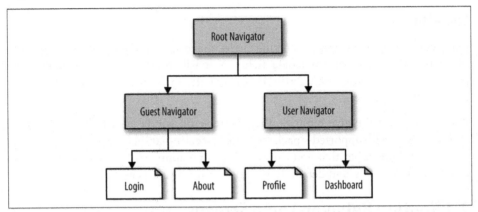

Figure 2-7. Nested navigation route structure

This example uses two navigators, one of which relies on tab navigation at the bottom of the screen in iOS. See Recipe 3.3 for more information on dealing with vector images.

The styles were pulled into a *styles.js* file in order to keep the navigation code focused on the problem at hand:

```
// styles.js
import {
  StyleSheet
} from 'react-native';

export const styles = StyleSheet.create({

  container: {
    paddingTop: 30,
    flex: 1
  },

  paragraphText: {
    fontSize: 16,
    lineHeight: 20,
  },

  titleText: {
    fontSize: 24,
    lineHeight: 30,
```

```
    },

    primaryButton: {
      padding: 20,
      backgroundColor: '#124473'
    },

    primaryButtonText: {
      color: '#FFF',
      textAlign: 'center',
    },

    altButton: {
      padding: 20,
      backgroundColor: '#23CdA4'
    },

    altButtonText: {
      color: '#FFF',
      textAlign: 'center',
    }
});
```

There are four screens in this example: AboutScreen, LoginScreen, Dash
boardScreen, and ProfileScreen. Each screen has its own file and is referenced in
App.js. The flow through the different screens can be seen in Figure 2-8.

```
// About Screen
import React, { Component } from 'react';
import {
  TouchableHighlight,
  View,
  Text
} from 'react-native';

import { styles } from './styles';

export default class AboutScreen extends Component<{}> {
  render() {
    return <View style={styles.container}>
      <Text style={styles.titleText} >About Screen</Text>
      <TouchableHighlight style={styles.primaryButton}
        onPress={this.props.navigation.goBack}
        <Text style={styles.primaryButtonText}>Go Back</Text>
      </TouchableHighlight>
    </View>
  }
}
```

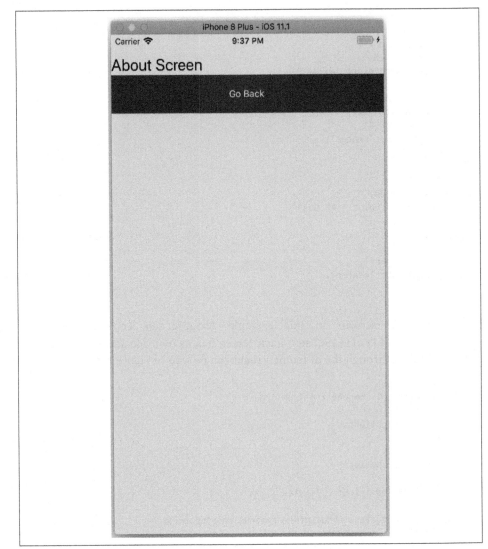

Figure 2-8. The About Screen

See Figure 2-9 for an example of the LoginScreen component.

Figure 2-9. The Login Screen

```
// Login Screen
import React, { Component } from 'react';
import {
  TouchableHighlight,
  View,
  Text
} from 'react-native';

import { styles } from './styles';

export default class LoginScreen extends Component<{}> {
  about = () => {
    const { navigate } = this.props.navigation
    navigate('about');
  }

  login = () => {
    const { navigate } = this.props.navigation;
    // some login code here...
    navigate('user', { user: { name: 'Sam Smith',
    email: 'sam.smith@example.com' } })
  }

  render() {
    return <View style={styles.container}>
      <Text style={styles.titleText} >Login Screen</Text>
      <TouchableHighlight style={styles.primaryButton}
      onPress={this.about}>
        <Text style={styles.primaryButtonText}>About</Text>
      </TouchableHighlight>
      <TouchableHighlight style={[styles.altButton, { marginTop: 20 } ]}
      onPress={this.login}>
        <Text style={styles.altButtonText}>Login</Text>
      </TouchableHighlight>
    </View>
  }
}
```

The Dashboard Screen component extracts user() state from the RootNavigator (Figure 2-10).

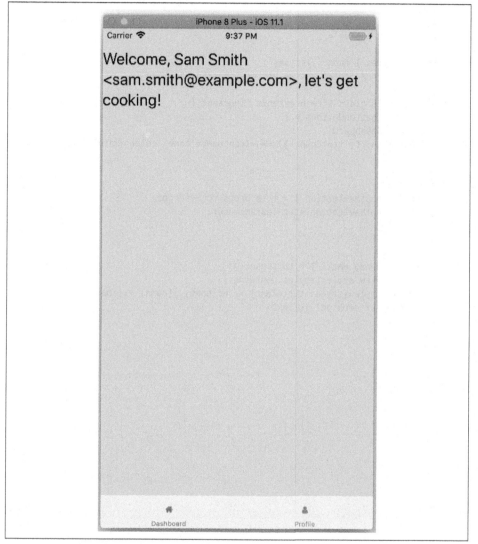

Figure 2-10. The Dashboard Screen

```
// Dashboard Screen
import React, { Component } from 'react';
import {
  View,
  Text
} from 'react-native';

import { styles } from './styles';
import Icon from 'react-native-vector-icons/FontAwesome';

export default class Screen extends Component {
  static navigationOptions = {
    title: 'Dashboard',
    tabBarIcon: ({ tintColor }) => <Icon name='home' color={tintColor} />
  }

  user() {
    const { rootNavigation } = this.props.screenProps;
    return rootNavigation.state.params.user;
  }

  render() {
    const { name, email } = this.user();
    return <View style={styles.container}>
      <Text style={styles.titleText} >{`Welcome, ${name} <${email}>,
      let's get cooking!`}</Text>
    </View>
  }
}
```

The Profile Screen (seen in Figure 2-11) demonstrates resetting the navigation state with the logout().

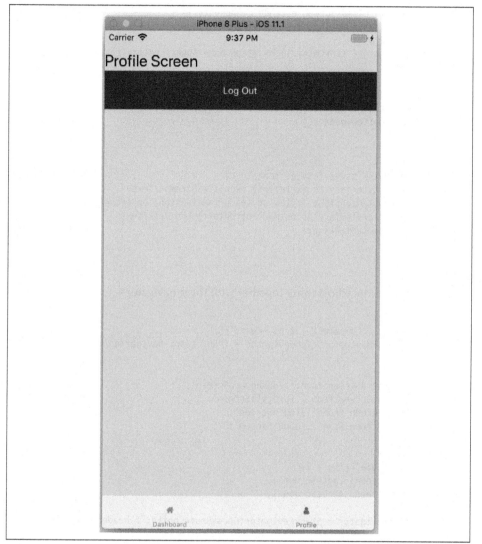

Figure 2-11. The Profile Screen

```
// Profile Screen
import React, { Component } from 'react';
import {
  TouchableHighlight,
  View,
  Text
} from 'react-native';
```

```
import Icon from 'react-native-vector-icons/FontAwesome';
import { styles } from './styles';

export default class Screen extends Component<{}> {
  static navigationOptions = {
    title: 'Profile',
    tabBarIcon: ({ tintColor }) => <Icon name='user' color={tintColor} />
  }

  logout = () => {
    const { rootNavigation } = this.props.screenProps;
    rootNavigation.goBack()
  }

  render() {
    return <View style={styles.container}>
      <Text style={styles.titleText} >Profile Screen</Text>
      <TouchableHighlight style={styles.primaryButton} onPress={this.logout}>
        <Text style={styles.primaryButtonText}>Log Out</Text>
      </TouchableHighlight>
    </View>
  }
}
```

Finally, *App.js* ties the whole thing together with three navigators:

```
// App.js
import React, { Component } from 'react';
import { StackNavigator, TabNavigator } from 'react-navigation';

// Screens
import DashboardScreen from './dashboardScreen';
import ProfileScreen from './profileScreen';
import LoginScreen from './loginScreen';
import AboutScreen from './aboutScreen';

// Navigators
const GuestRouteConfig = {
  login: { screen: LoginScreen },
  about: { screen: AboutScreen },
}
const GuestNavigator = StackNavigator(GuestRouteConfig, { headerMode: 'none'} );

const UserRouteConfig = {
  dashboard: { screen: DashboardScreen },
  profile:   { screen: ProfileScreen },
}

const UserNavigator = TabNavigator(UserRouteConfig, {
activeTintColor: '#125000' });

// Pass the RootNavigator down to the UserNavigator:
const WrappedNavigator = ({ navigation }) => <UserNavigator
```

```
    screenProps={ { rootNavigation: navigation } } />

  const RootRouteConfig = {
    guest: { screen: GuestNavigator },
    user: { screen: WrappedNavigator },
  }

  export default StackNavigator(RootRouteConfig, { headerMode: 'none' });
```

Discussion

Even though this is a lengthy example, it is a very common pattern and worth exploring. You will notice that the UserNavigator is actually wrapped in a *higher order component*, which passes the RootNavigator down as an additional screenProp called rootNavigation. This parameter is critical for passing successful login parameters down to the UserNavigator and enables the ProfileScreen to trigger a logout, resetting the RootNavigator to a default state.

See Also

React Navigation works very well with libraries like *Redux* and the *ApolloClient* for handling client/server interactions. The React Navigation Redux Integration guide (*http://bit.ly/2nK6J3J*) provides a starting point. React Navigation isn't the only navigation library available to React Native developers. React Native Navigation (*http://bit.ly/2E8WrAi*) is a well-maintained alternative.

2.5 Using Redux for Global State Management in Redux

The moment you find yourself with more than one screen, state management decisions will need to be made. Whether you decide to follow a flux-inspired architecture like Redux or to implement your own global storage with AsyncStorage, the question of how to keep the data that matters locally decoupled from broader state management will enter the picture.

Problem

How do you manage state components without creating bidirectional dependencies? These problems are everywhere in application design. A common case is a long-running task that can be interrupted by a user, but also must announce its completion. Enter global state management with Redux. This example app will store a password based on four word-tiles. Once logged in, users will be able to set some secret text. This app enables a user to:

1. Set a tile-based password and log in (like a pin-pad)

2. Set some secret text

3. Log out

4. Log in with the password

5. Reset the application state

6. Correct their login attempt and retry

Solution

First we need a few libraries for Redux and React to work together. I also use `redux-logger` in development mode to log all state transitions in the React remote debugger.

Install `react-redux`, `redux`, and `redux-logger` (optional):

```
$>npm i --save react-redux
$>npm i --save redux
$>npm i --save redux-logger
```

The project folder structure looks like this:

```
App.js
reduxStore.js
...
src
├── actions.js
├── appContainer.js
├── components
│   ├── tile.js
│   └── tileMap.js
├── constants.js
├── loginForm.js
├── myHome.js
├── reducers.js
├── setPassword.js
├── styles.js
└── types.js
```

> See Recipe 1.3 for examples on organizing your project files. Given that this example focuses on Redux, I've tried to limit the number of files and folders. In a larger application, screen-based (e.g., *home/*, *login/*) or type (e.g., *reducers/*, *actions/*) folders are more appropriate.

The same TileMap component can be used to set a password, as in Figure 2-12.

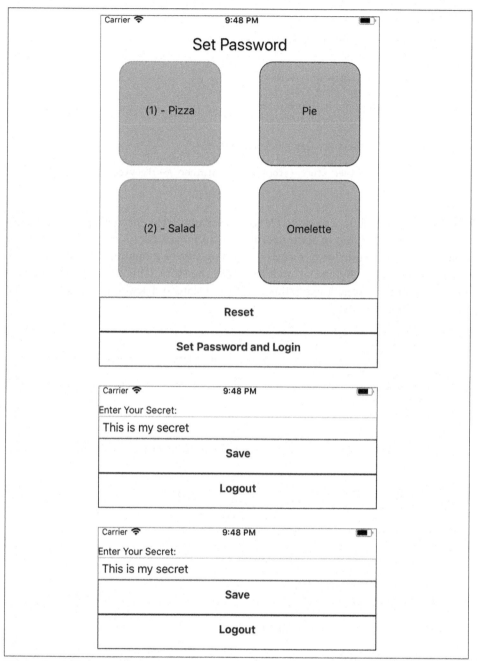

Figure 2-12. Users can access a secret message after setting a visual password by selecting a set of tiles

Redux integration

The *App.js* file is devoted entirely to the redux integration:

```
// App.js
import React, { Component } from 'react';
import AppContainer from './src/appContainer';
import { Provider } from 'react-redux';
import store from './reduxStore';

export default class App extends Component<{}> {
  render() {
    return <Provider store={store}><AppContainer /></Provider>
  }
}
```

The `store` is defined in a separate file so that it can be referenced globally. This is not commonly required, but in some exceptional circumstances (particularly when there is no remote backend store), access to the state from actions can be necessary. The `redux-logger` is configured as middleware in the store. This library is an optional piece of additional functionality that will log all state and action changes to the web browser debugger console:

```
// reduxStore.js
import * as reducers from './src/reducers'
import { createStore, applyMiddleware, combineReducers, compose} from 'redux';
import logger from 'redux-logger';
export default createStore(
  combineReducers(reducers),
  applyMiddleware(logger)
);
```

The `AppContainer` relies on the `appState` reducer to determine which screens to render:

```
// src/appContainer.js
import ActionCreators from './actions';
import { bindActionCreators } from 'redux';
import { connect } from 'react-redux';

import SetPassword from './setPassword';
import LoginForm from './loginForm';
import MyHome from './myHome';
import { styles } from './styles';

class AppContainer extends Component {

  renderLoginMessage() {
    return <Text style={styles.loginMessage}>
      {this.props.appState.loginMessage}
    </Text>
  }
```

```
    render() {
      const { isLoggedIn, loginMessage, isPasswordSet } = this.props.appState;
      return <View style={styles.container}>
        { isLoggedIn && <MyHome /> }
        { !isLoggedIn && !isPasswordSet && <SetPassword /> }
        { !isLoggedIn && isPasswordSet && <LoginForm /> }
        { loginMessage && this.renderLoginMessage() }
      </View>
    }
  }

  export default connect(
    ({ appState }) => { return { appState } },
    (dispatch) => bindActionCreators(ActionCreators, dispatch)
  )(AppContainer);
```

Actions and types

Redux applications naturally produce a listing of supported events that the application must support. There are a number of libraries that aim to reduce the amount of boilerplate, but in the interest of simplicity, I've decided to rely on the minimum number of external dependencies:

```
// src/types.js
export const LOGIN = 'LOGIN';
export const LOGOUT = 'LOGOUT';
export const RESET = 'RESET';
export const SET_PASSWORD_AND_LOGIN = 'SET_PASSWORD_AND_LOGIN';
export const SET_SECRET = 'SET_SECRET';
export const SET_LOGIN_MESSAGE = 'SET_LOGIN_MESSAGE';
```

These actions are exposed to the entire application as *ActionCreators*, which can be used to dispatch events that the *reducers* can choose to respond to. ActionCreators can sometimes also handle some delegation to global business logic. Instead of relying on a backend service for user authentication, I've referred to the store in order to extract the user state and trigger the correct action. This example demonstrates how *actions* don't always map one-to-one with *types* and *stores*:

```
// src/actions.
import * as types from './types';
// Used for authentication
import store from '../reduxStore';

function setSecret(secret) {
  return {
    type: types.SET_SECRET,
    secret
  }
}
```

```
function setPasswordAndLogin(password) {
  return {
    type: types.SET_PASSWORD_AND_LOGIN,
    password
  }
}

function attemptLogin(password) {
  const { user } = store.getState();
  return (user.password === password) ? { type: types.LOGIN } : {
    type: types.SET_LOGIN_MESSAGE,
    loginMessage: "Login Incorrect"
  }
}

function reset() {
  return {
    type: types.RESET,
  }
}

function logout() {
  return {
    type: types.LOGOUT,
  }
}

function setLoginMessage(message) {
  return {
    type: types.SET_LOGIN_MESSAGE,
    message
  }
}

export default ActionCreators = {
  setSecret,
  setPasswordAndLogin,
  attemptLogin,
  reset,
  logout,
  setLoginMessage,
}
```

Reducers

We will rely on a single store with two reducers, an `appState` and a `user` reducer. Unlike a more common TODO example, this example demonstrates multiple reducers and how actions can be used for global state management.

Both reducers are exported from *src/reducers.js*. A createReducer() function provides some syntactic sugar for avoiding pure case statements in the reducer. Notice how the appState and user reducers both respond to types.RESET and types.SET_PASSWORD_AND_LOGIN. Also consider that the reducers do not determine whether the person should log in; they merely process the event and return the appropriate state transformation to their part of the store:

```
// src/reducers.js
import * as types from './types'
// Helper function for avoiding switch() statements (commonly viewed
// as a code smell) in reducers:
function createReducer(initialState, handlers) {
  return function reducer(state = initialState, action) {
    if (handlers.hasOwnProperty(action.type)) {
      return handlers[action.type](state, action);
    } else {
      return state;
    }
  }
}

export const user = createReducer({ password: null, secret: null }, {
  [types.RESET](state, { } ) {
    return { password: null, secret: null }
  },
  [types.SET_SECRET](state, { secret } ) {
    return { ...state, secret }
  },
  [types.SET_PASSWORD_AND_LOGIN](state, { password } ) {
    return { ...state, password };
  },
});

const initialAppState = {
  loginMessage: null,
  isLoggedIn: false,
  isPasswordSet: false
};

export const appState = createReducer(initialAppState, {
  [types.LOGOUT](state, {} ) {
    return { ...state, isLoggedIn: false }
  },
  [types.LOGIN](state, {} ) {
    return { ...state, isLoggedIn: true, loginMessage: null }
  },
  [types.SET_LOGIN_MESSAGE](state, { loginMessage } ) {
    return { ...state, loginMessage }
  },
  [types.RESET](state, { } ) {
    return { ...initialAppState };
```

```
    },
    [types.SET_PASSWORD_AND_LOGIN](state, { } ) {
      return { isLoggedIn: true, isPasswordSet: true, loginMessage: null }
    },

});
```

Styles and constants

Most of the application styles have been centralized into a global *src/styles.js* file:

```
// src/styles.js
import {
  StyleSheet
} from 'react-native';

export const styles = StyleSheet.create({
  loginMessage: {
    margin: 10,
    fontSize: 16,
    padding: 10
  },

  rootContainer: {
    flex: 1,
    paddingTop: 30,
    backgroundColor: '#FFF',
  },

  buttonGroup: {
    marginTop: 10,
  },

  container: {
    paddingTop: 30,
    flex: 1
  },

  title: {
    fontSize: 24,
    lineHeight: 30,
    textAlign: 'center',
  },

  tileRow: {
    flexWrap: 'wrap',
    flexDirection: 'row',
    justifyContent: 'space-around' ,
  },

  button: {
    borderWidth: 1,
    borderColor: '#333',
```

```
    borderStyle: 'solid',
    height: 50,
  },

  buttonText: {
    color: '#144595',
    fontWeight: 'bold',
    fontSize: 16,
    padding: 10,
    textAlign: 'center',
  },
});
```

The *src/constants.js* file provides a central list of TILES that will be used for rendering the <TileMap /> component, whether for setting a password or for logging in:

```
// src/constants.js
export const TILES = {
  'Pizza': {    text: 'Pizza',    value: 'pizza',    index: null,
  isActive: false },
  'Pie': {      text: 'Pie',      value: 'pie',      index: null,
  isActive: false },
  'Salad': {    text: 'Salad',    value: 'salad',    index: null,
  isActive: false },
  'Omelette': { text: 'Omelette', value: 'omelette', index: null,
  isActive: false },
}
```

The Tile and TileMap components

The *src/components/* folder contains a few components that were designed to function without any knowledge of Redux. The <Tile /> component is a *pure function* that simply returns a JSX transformation of the tile props:

```
// src/components/tile.js
import React, { Component } from 'react';
import {
  StyleSheet,
  TouchableHighlight,
  Text
} from 'react-native'

export default function Tile({ text, id, isActive, onPress }) {
  const activeStyle = isActive ? { borderColor: '#F00' } : null;
  return <TouchableHighlight style={[styles.tile, activeStyle ]}
  onPress={() => onPress(id) }>
    <Text style={styles.tileText}>{text}</Text>
  </TouchableHighlight>
}
```

```
const styles = StyleSheet.create({
  container: {
    flex: 1,
    paddingTop: 30,
    backgroundColor: '#FFF',
  },

  headerText: {
    color: '#144595',
    fontSize: 16,
    fontWeight: 'bold',
    textAlign: 'center',
  },

  header: {
    borderBottomWidth: 1,
    borderBottomColor: '#222',
    borderStyle: 'solid',
  },

  tileText: {
    fontSize: 16,
    textAlign: 'center',
    marginTop: 60,
  },

  tile: {
    width: 150,
    height: 150,
    alignItems: 'center',
    backgroundColor: '#CCC',
    borderRadius: 20,
    borderColor: '#222',
    borderWidth: 1,
    borderStyle: 'solid',
    margin: 10,
  }

})
```

The `<TileMap />` component renders a collection of `<Tile />` components and orchestrates their state and tap events. Each `<Tile />` provides an `onTileChange` handler that returns a password as a string. `<Tile />` will render anything in `this.props.children` that the parent component may want to include, such as special buttons.

Here's an implementation of the `<TileMap />`:

```
// src/components/tileMap.js
import React, { Component } from 'react';
import {
  View,
```

```
    TouchableHighlight,
    Text
} from 'react-native';

import Tile from './tile';
import { TILES  } from '../constants';
import { styles } from '../styles';

function computePassword(tiles) {
  let password = []
  Object.keys(tiles).forEach( (key) => {
    const tile = tiles[key];
    if (tile.isActive) {
      password[tile.index] = tile.value;
    }
  });
  // chop off the 0
  return password.slice(1).join('-');
}

export default class TileMap extends Component<{}> {

  constructor(props) {
    super(props);
    this.state = { tiles: {...TILES}, index: 0 }
  }

  reset = () => {
    this.setState( { tiles: {...TILES}, index: 0 });
    this.props.onTileChanged(computePassword(this.state.tiles));
  }

  setPassword = () => {
    this.props.setPasswordAndLogin(this.state.tiles);
  }

  tilePressed = (id) => {
  if (this.state.tiles[id].isActive) { return; }
  this.setState((prevState) => {
    const tiles = prevState.tiles;
    const newIndex = prevState.index + 1;
    const currentTile = tiles[id];
    tiles[id] = { ...currentTile,
      index: newIndex,
      text: `(${newIndex}) - ${currentTile.text}`,
      isActive: true
    }
    return {...tiles, index: newIndex }
  });
  this.props.onTileChanged(computePassword(this.state.tiles));
}
```

```
    render() {
      return <View>
        <View style={styles.tileRow}>
          {Object.keys(this.state.tiles).map( (key) => {
              const tile = this.state.tiles[key];
              return <Tile {...tile} id={key} key={key} onPress={this.tilePressed} />
              }
          )}
        </View>
        <View style={styles.buttonGroup}>
          <TouchableHighlight style={styles.button} onPress={this.reset}>
            <Text style={styles.buttonText}>Reset</Text>
          </TouchableHighlight>
          {this.props.children}
        </View>
      </View>
    }
  }
```

Application screens

Now that we have all the components and their Redux dependencies, we can look at
the screens that trigger state changes. These screens are considered *presentational
components*, meaning that they trigger *actions* and are accepting *props* from the *store*.
These components are imported from <AppContainer />.

The first screen the user sees is the <SetPassword /> screen. Notice that the <Tile
Map /> is used and the this.state.password value is sent as a message to the set
PasswordAndLogin() action creator:

```
// src/setPassword.js
import React, { Component } from 'react';
import {
  View,
  TouchableHighlight,
  Text
} from 'react-native'

import ActionCreators from './actions'
import { bindActionCreators } from 'redux'
import { connect } from 'react-redux'
import TileMap from './components/tileMap'
import { styles } from './styles'

class SetPassword extends Component<{}> {

  constructor(props) {
    super(props);
    this.state = { password: null }
  }
```

```
    onTileChanged = (password) => {
      this.setState( { password });
    }

    setPassword = () => {
      this.props.setPasswordAndLogin(this.state.password);
    }

    render() {
      return <View>
        <Text style={styles.title}>Set Password</Text>
        <TileMap onTileChanged={this.onTileChanged}>
          <TouchableHighlight style={styles.button} onPress={this.setPassword}>
            <Text style={styles.buttonText}>Set Password and Login</Text>
          </TouchableHighlight>
        </TileMap>
      </View>
    }
  }

export default connect(
  ({ user }) => { return { user } },
  (dispatch) => bindActionCreators(ActionCreators, dispatch)
)(SetPassword);
```

When a user `isLoggedIn`, the `<MyHome />` component is rendered. This may appear to be a contrived example, but it demonstrates the difference between local and global state. The `user` reducer is maintaining the `secret`, but only after `setSecret()` is called, triggering a state transformation in the `user` reducer. Notice that the component does not know what `logout()` does; it merely sends the message and relies on the `appState` reducer:

```
// src/myHome.js
import React, { Component } from 'react';
import {
  TextInput,
  TouchableHighlight,
  View,
  Text
} from 'react-native';
import { bindActionCreators } from 'redux';
import { connect } from 'react-redux';
import Tile from './components/tile';
import { TILES } from './constants';
import { styles } from './styles';

class MyHome extends Component<{}> {
  constructor(props) {
    super(props);
    this.state = { secret: props.user.secret || '' }
  }
```

```
saveSecret = () => {
  this.props.setSecret(this.state.secret);
}

logout = () => {
  this.props.logout();
}

render() {
  return <View>
    <Text>Enter Your Secret:</Text>
    <TextInput value={this.state.secret}
      style={{borderWidth: 1, borderColor: "#CCC", padding: 5, }}
      onChangeText={(secret) => { this.setState({ secret }) }} />
    <TouchableHighlight style={styles.button} onPress={this.saveSecret}>
      <Text style={styles.buttonText}>Save</Text>
    </TouchableHighlight>
    <TouchableHighlight style={styles.button} onPress={this.logout}>
      <Text style={styles.buttonText}>Logout</Text>
    </TouchableHighlight>
  </View>
  }
}

export default connect(
  ({ user }) => ({ user }),
  (dispatch) => bindActionCreators(ActionCreators, dispatch)
)(MyHome);
```

The `<LoginForm />` component is almost identical to the `<SetPassword />` component in structure, but it maps components to a different set of *action creators* for handling account reset and user login. This is an example of repurposing the `<TileMap />` component for a completely different use case:

```
import React, { Component } from 'react';
import {
  View,
  TouchableHighlight,
  Text
} from 'react-native';

import ActionCreators from './actions';
import { bindActionCreators } from 'redux';
import { connect } from 'react-redux';
import TileMap from './components/tileMap';
import { styles } from './styles';

class LoginForm extends Component<{}> {

  constructor(props) {
    super(props);
```

```
      this.state = { password: null }
    }

    onTileChanged = (password) => {
      this.setState( { password });
    }

    resetAccount = () => {
      this.props.reset();
    }

    login = () => {
      this.props.attemptLogin(this.state.password);
    }

    render() {
      return <View>
        <Text style={styles.title}>Login</Text>
        <TileMap onTileChanged={this.onTileChanged}>
          <TouchableHighlight style={styles.button} onPress={this.login}>
            <Text style={styles.buttonText}>Login</Text>
          </TouchableHighlight>
          <TouchableHighlight style={styles.button} onPress={this.resetAccount}>
            <Text style={styles.buttonText}>Reset Account</Text>
          </TouchableHighlight>
        </TileMap>
      </View>
    }

}

export default connect(
  ({ user }) => ({ user }),
  (dispatch) => bindActionCreators(ActionCreators, dispatch)
)(LoginForm);
```

Discussion

Redux can be intimidating if you are new to JavaScript. This is because the library is *simple*, but not *simplistic*: the programming concepts are profound and require some experience to grasp, but there are few of them and they elegantly support one another. It's helpful to think of Redux as a software design pattern and a JavaScript library at the same time. Adopting one without the other will leave a sour taste in your mouth.

Even if you decide to use another state management library, you will probably face a library, like react-navigation, with Redux under the hood. Understanding the programmer attitudes around mutable state, pure functions, composition, and higher order functions will bring state management in the React ecosystem into focus.

I would not be able to do justice to the fantastic Redux documentation (*http://redux.js.org*) and the incredible wealth of free video tutorials (*https://egghead.io/courses/getting-started-with-redux*) (including some of my own on YouTube (*https://youtu.be/3msLwu25SQY*)). However, there are three principles worth keeping in mind as we implement Redux in our app:

> *Single source of truth:* The state of your whole application is stored in an object tree within a single store. ... *State is read-only:* The only way to change the state is to emit an action, an object describing what happened. ... *Changes are made with pure functions:* To specify how the state tree is transformed by actions, you write pure reducers.
>
> —redux.js.org, *Three Principles*

See Also

redux-thunk and redux-saga provide some helpful extensions to the Redux architecture for dealing with any asynchronous calls. Given that your app is likely going to talk to a server or read sensor data, asynchronous actions are inevitable.

CHAPTER 3

Style and Design

Most of the work involved in making a native app feel polished comes from having well-designed components that can communicate a strong visual identity within the user-experience conventions of the platform. For example, iOS applications tend to rely on bottom tab navigation. The lefthand drawer or the *Snackbar* notifications are typically seen in Android.

Building a cross-platform application will probably mean making certain design choices that balance user experience, platform conventions, and technical complexity. These tips should help you make those choices more easily.

3.1 Composing Stylesheets

Maintaining a growing stylesheet is a challenge in any web application. Native applications are no different. Fortunately, React components allow us to create a unit of code that combines everything required for a user interface element to render correctly.

In the last few years, the debate around how to organize web styles has led to all sorts of semantics for describing what something is supposed to look like. Whether you are familiar with *Object-Oriented CSS*, *SMACCS*, *Tachyons*, or *BEM*, any of these design choices rely on the language's ability to compose stylesheet declarations.

React Native does not support CSS. CSS is a language for describing how something looks, with syntax that reduces the effort in defining common styles. This section illustrates how we can achieve many of the features of CSS using simple JavaScript declarations.

Problem

How do we reuse as many styles as possible and keep the application's look and feel consistent?

Solution

All applications will have a common set of applicable fonts, colors, and component styles. These might include how rounded a button corner should be, or what the appropriate padding should be between typographic elements. I like to keep these bits of style information in a *styles.js* file in my project root with key sections that will broadly define the aesthetic of my application:

1. Color Palette
2. Typography Choices
3. Global Styles

Inheriting styles

Here's an example of what a *styles.js* file might look like:

```
import { Dimensions } from 'react-native';
const { width, height } = Dimensions.get('window');

// COLOR
export const colors = {
  PRIMARY: '#005D64',
  SECONDARY: '#CA3F27',
}

// TYPOGRAPHY
const scalingFactors = {
  small: 40,
  normal: 30,
  big: 20,
}

export const fontSizes = {
  H1: {
    fontSize: width / scalingFactors.big,
    lineHeight: (width / scalingFactors.big) * 1.3,
  },

  P: {
    fontSize: width / scalingFactors.normal,
    lineHeight: (width / scalingFactors.normal) * 1.3,
  },
```

```
    SMALL: {
      fontSize: width / scalingFactors.small,
    },
}

// GLOBAL STYLES
export const globalStyles = {
  textHeader: {...fontSizes.H1,
    color: colors.PRIMARY,
    paddingTop: 20,
    fontWeight: 'bold',
  },
}
```

The `textHeader` component illustrates a classic form of composition. It relies on the `fontSizes.H1` key as a basis for the `textHeader`. If we need to change the overall size of the primary header in our application, we need only change the scaling factors to see these adjustments happen everywhere.

By importing the `Dimensions` library from React Native, we can perform some simple math operations in our definition of these `fontSizes`, ensuring that the typography *feels* the same across platforms and device sizes.[1]

The biggest benefit to this approach is that all the styles are defined using the same programming language we use to build the rest of the application.

Overriding inline styles

With global styles defined, they can be referenced in your own flavor of the base components. For example, here is a definition for `<TextHeading />` and `<SecondaryTextHeading />` components:

```
import React from 'react';
import {
  Text,
} from 'react-native';
import { globalStyles, colors } from '../styles';

export function TextHeading (props) {
  return <Text style={globalStyles.textHeader} >{props.children}</Text>
}

export function SecondaryTextHeading(props) {
  return <Text
    style={[globalStyles.textHeader, { color: colors.SECONDARY } ]} >
      {props.children}
```

---

1 See Chapter 9 of *Learning React Native*, 1E (O'Reilly Media) for more about responsive design and font sizes.

```
    </Text>
  }
```

In the preceding example, rather than implement a class that extends `React.Compo` `nent`, I use a shorthand for a pure function—a function with no side effects—which supports two JSX components. This syntax provides a hint to the developer that this function will not have any local state.

The `<SecondaryTextHeading />` component overrides the `color` declaration with a `style` array attribute. Each item in the array is merged together, with the last item in the array overriding any previous declarations. The `style` attribute in this case will be:

```
{
  fontSize: width / scalingFactors.big,
  lineHeight: (width / scalingFactors.big) * 1.3,
  color: colors.SECONDARY,
  paddingTop: 20,
  fontWeight: 'bold',
}
```

See Also

There are some great component libraries in the React Native ecosystem. react-native-elements (*http://bit.ly/2Embj1R*) provides an excellent set of cross-platform components with some of the most common components. NativeBase (*https://native base.io/*) accomplishes the same goals with a more featureful component library. These libraries are a great way of ensuring that your app will be functional and consistent.

react-native-material-kit (*http://bit.ly/2E9d4Aa*) aims to provide a complete component library based on Google's Material Design (*https://material.io/*).

If you find yourself customizing every component, you might be better off developing your own component library.

3.2 Building Flexible Layouts with Flexbox

Your app will run on a number of different form factors and device sizes. This means that setting up a pixel-based design will result in a lot of testing and per-device rework. Avoid most of those headaches by using a flexbox layout.

Problem

How do you build a flexible layout system that will work with different device sizes? Using just a handful of style declarations we can build complex views like the one in Figure 3-1.

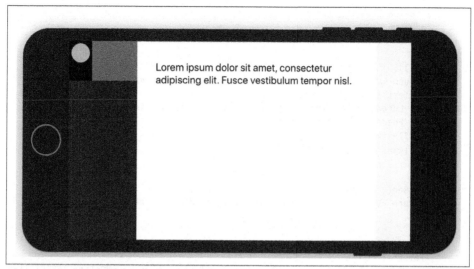

Figure 3-1. A 3-column flexbox layout

Solution

The layout in Figure 3-1 was rendered using this simple component. While I would recommend using the StyleSheet class for performance and reusability, writing the styles inline helps illustrate how each parent <View /> configures the flow direction of the child <View />:

```
import React, { Component } from 'react';
import {
  Text,
  View
} from 'react-native';

export default class ThreeColumns extends Component {

  sidebar() {
    const avatarStyle = {
      width: 40,
      height: 40,
      borderRadius: 40,
      justifyContent: 'center',
      backgroundColor: '#A0'
    }
    return <View style={{ flex: 0.2,  backgroundColor: '#333' }}>
      <View style={{ flex: 0.2,    backgroundColor: '#666',
      flexDirection: 'row' }}>
        <View style={{ width: 50, padding: 5, backgroundColor: '#000' }}>
          <View style={avatarStyle} />
        </View>
      </View>
    </View>
```

```
        <View style={{ flex: 0.8 }} />
      </View>
  }

  body() {
    return <View style={{ flex: 0.5, backgroundColor: '#FFF' }}>
      <Text style={{padding: 40, fontSize: 22}}>
        Lorem ipsum dolor sit amet, consectetur adipiscing elit.
        Fusce vestibulum tempor nisl.
      </Text>
    </View>
  }

  rightBar() {
    return <View style={{ flex: 0.1, backgroundColor: '#FFA' }}></View>
  }

  render() {
    return (
      <View style={{ flexDirection: 'row', flex: 1, backgroundColor: '#FFF' }}>
        {this.sidebar()}
        {this.body()}
        {this.rightBar()}
      </View>
    );
  }
}
```

Flex and FlexDirection

The main render() function wraps a sidebar(), body(), and rightBar() component with a flexDirection: "row" style attribute. The flexDirection will dictate
whether block elements should stack vertically or horizontally. By default, a <View />
will stack vertically. The default flexDirection in React Native is *column* and not *row*
(like in CSS).

In this case, we want our outer container to *flow* like a row: with the sidebar, body,
and rightBar appearing next to each other. The flex value indicates the relative size
of the container. There are two commonly used conventions for flex values: 1 or 10.
In this case, the outer view has a container size of 1. sidebar() will take up 20% of
the component size with a flex value of 0.2. The body() function will return a
<View /> with a flex value of 0.5, accounting for 50% of the view. The remaining
rightBar() will fill 10%.

Other attributes

There are some other flexbox style declarations for handling alignment and what to do with excess space in the layout. Once you have the right blocks in place, use `justifyContent` and `alignItems` to position the child elements. Flexbox views also work well with pixel-based views like the `avatarStyle` in the preceding code.

Discussion

Flexbox layouts originated in the web design community as a mechanism for handling the challenge of an ever-changing browser window. Fortunately for web developers, you are probably already familiar with the CSS implementation of flexbox, so you should have little trouble adjusting to React Native's implementation.

See Also

The React Native documentation provides a helpful guide for laying out flexbox views (*http://bit.ly/2ENNIoE*).

3.3 Importing Image Vectors and Icons

Your app will start coming alive once you include icons and other design cues. Fortunately we can use libraries like `react-native-vector-icons` (*http://bit.ly/2FUwKUK*).

Problem

How do you decide the best way to display vector images in your application?

Solution

Working with images and binaries is easily done with `require()` statements, but vectors and icons are special. They do not render out of the box in Android or iOS.

Different solutions exist depending on whether you have a number of vectors files, the complexity of the design, whether or not there are multiple colors in the design, and if you need to target a number of platforms.

Convert to images

The simplest solution in some cases is simply to convert the file into a rasterized file format, like PNG or JPG. The React Native packager is smart enough to detect these dependencies and bundle them together. In order for the file to render correctly for different screen densities, it's helpful to provide alternative versions of the same file.

In this case, I have a vector of a lightbulb, *bulb.svg*, which has been converted into a number of different pixel density equivalent images:

```
components
└── images
    ├── bulb.svg
    ├── bulb@1x.android.png
    ├── bulb@1x.ios.png
    ├── bulb@2x.android.png
    ├── bulb@2x.ios.png
    ├── bulb@3x.android.png
    ├── bulb@3x.ios.png
    ├── bulb@4x.android.png
    └── index.js
```

Vector editing programs like Adobe Illustrator provide an "Export to Screens" function, making exporting different pixel densities easy, as shown in Figure 3-2.

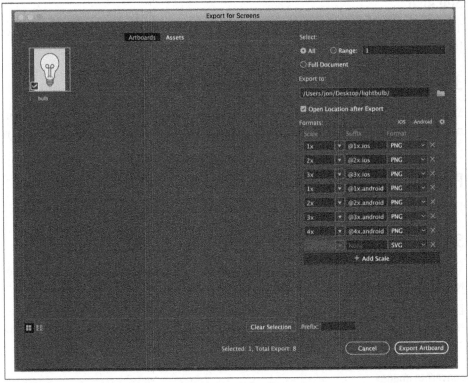

Figure 3-2. Export to Screens capability in Adobe Illustrator

The *index.js* file uses a `require()` statement that can infer the correct image and platform to load:

```
import React, { Component } from 'react';
import { Image } from 'react-native';

export const Bulb = () => <Image source={require('./bulb.png')} />
```

In the main application, you can now reference the image as though it were any other React component:

```
import { Bulb } from './components/images'
export default class App extends Component<{}> {
  render() {
    return (
        <View style={{flex: 1, justifyContent: 'center',
        alignItems: 'center' }}>
        <Bulb />
      </View>
    );
  }
}
```

There are a couple of solutions to vectors: converting them to SVG markup and using a library or converting them to fonts.

Drawing an SVG

`react-native-vector-icons` provides a set of React components for describing an SVG using React Native components. At the time of this writing, certain attributes such as `clip-path` are partially supported. This approach requires essentially redrawing the icon in the application.

The same lightbulb can be exported as the following SVG file:

```
<?xml version="1.0" encoding="UTF-8"?>
<svg xmlns="http://www.w3.org/2000/svg" id="Layer_1" data-name="Layer 1"
viewBox="0 0 86 114">
    <defs>
        <style>.cls-1{fill:#dcdfe1;}.cls-1,.cls-4,.cls-5{stroke:#555e65;
        stroke-miterlimit:10;
        stroke-width:2px;}.cls-2{fill:#fff;}.cls-3{fill:#faf7de;}
        .cls-4,.cls-5{fill:none;}
                        .cls-4{opacity:0.5;}
        </style>
    </defs>
    <title>bulb</title>
    <g id="Lightbulb">
        <ellipse class="cls-1" cx="43" cy="96.61" rx="6.77" ry="5.42" />
        <ellipse class="cls-1" cx="43" cy="92.55" rx="10.16" ry="5.42" />
        <ellipse class="cls-1" cx="43" cy="88.48" rx="10.16" ry="5.42" />
        <ellipse class="cls-1" cx="43" cy="84.42" rx="10.16" ry="5.42" />
        <path class="cls-2" d="M70.08,39.06A27.09,27.09,0,1,0,23.44,58,20,20,
                        0,0,1,29, 72.21v3.41c0,5.61,6.52,10.16,14,
                        10.16s14-4.55,14-10.16v-3.4a19.94,19.94,0,0,1,
```

```
                                5.52-14.16A26.78,26.78,0,0,0,70.08,39.06Z" />
        <path class="cls-3" d="M44.5,85.1C38.15,85.1,33,81.45,33,77V73.57a22.24,
                                22.24,0,0,0-6.45-15.62,25,25,0,0,1,
                                16-42.52q.9-.06,1.82-.06a25.08,25.08,0,0,1,25,
                                25.05A24.83,24.83,0,0,1,62.27,58,22,22,0,0,0,56,
                                73.57V77C56,81.45,50.85,85.1,44.5,85.1Z" />
        <path class="cls-4" d="M34.2,79c0-3,3.94-5.42,8.8-5.42S51.8,76,51.8,79" />
        <path class="cls-5" d="M50.45,42.44h.15A4.62,4.62,0,0,0,46,
                                47.18V52h4.45a4.77,4.77,0,0,0,4.74-4.78v0A4.76,
                                4.76,0,0,0,50.45,42.44Z" />
        <path class="cls-5" d="M35.55,42.44h-.15A4.62,4.62,0,0,1,40,
                                47.18V52H35.55a4.77,4.77,0,0,1-4.74-4.78v0A4.76,
                                4.76,0,0,1,35.55,42.44Z" />
        <polyline class="cls-5" points="46 79 46 52 40 52 40 79" />
        <path class="cls-5" d="M70.08,39.06A27.09,27.09,0,1,0,23.44,58,20,20,
                                0,0,1,29,72.21v3.41c0,5.61,6.52,10.16,14,
                                10.16s14-4.55,14-10.16v-3.4a19.94,19.94,0,0,1,
                                5.52-14.16A26.78,26.78,0,0,0,70.08,39.06Z" />
    </g>
</svg>
```

Because `react-native-vector-icons` supports a subset of the SVG specification, it would need to be redrawn without the style reference:

```
import React, { Component } from 'react';
import Svg,{
    Ellipse,
    Path,
    Polyline,
} from 'react-native-svg';

export default function() {
  return <Svg height="130" width="100">
    <Ellipse cx="43" cy="96.61" rx="6.77" ry="5.42"   fill="#dcdfe1"
    stroke="#555e65" strokeWidth="2" />
    <Ellipse cx="43" cy="92.55" rx="10.16" ry="5.42"  fill="#dcdfe1"
    stroke="#555e65" strokeWidth="2"/>
    <Ellipse cx="43" cy="88.48" rx="10.16" ry="5.42"  fill="#dcdfe1"
    stroke="#555e65" strokeWidth="2"/>
    <Ellipse cx="43" cy="84.42" rx="10.16" ry="5.42"  fill="#dcdfe1"
    stroke="#555e65" strokeWidth="2"/>
    <Path fill="#Faf7de"  d="M70.08,39.06A27.09,27.09,0,1,0,23.44,58,20,20,0,
                    0,1,29,72.21v3.41c0,5.61,6.52,10.16,14,10.16s14-4.55,
                    14-10.16v-3.4a19.94,19.94,0,0,1,
                    5.52-14.16A26.78,26.78,0,0,0,70.08,39.06Z" />
    <Path fill="none" d="M44.5,85.1C38.15,85.1,33,81.45,33,77V73.57a22.24,22.24,
                    0,0,0-6.45-15.62,25,25,0,0,1,16-42.52q.9-.06,
                    1.82-.06a25.08,25.08,0,0,1,25,25.05A24.83,24.83,
                    0,0,1,62.27,58,22,22,0,0,0,56,73.57V77C56,81.45,50.85,
                    85.1,44.5,85.1Z" />
    <Path fill="none" d="M34.2,79c0-3,3.94-5.42,8.8-5.42S51.8,76,51.8,79" />
    <Path stroke="#555e65" strokeWidth="2" fill="none" d="M50.45,42.44h.15A4.62,
                    4.62,0,0,0,46,47.18V52h4.45a4.77,4.77,
```

```
                    0,0,0,4.74-4.78v0A4.76,4.76,0,0,0,
                    50.45,42.44Z" />
  <Path stroke="#555e65" strokeWidth="2" fill="none" d="M35.55,42.44h-.15A4.62,
                    4.62,0,0,1,40,47.18V52H35.55a4.77,4.77,0,0,
                    1-4.74-4.78v0A4.76,4.76,0,0,1,35.55,42.44Z" />
  <Polyline stroke="#555e65" strokeWidth="2" fill="none"
  points="46 79 46 52 40 52 40 79" />
  <Path stroke="#555e65" strokeWidth="2" fill="none" d="M70.08,39.06A27.09,
                    27.09,0,1,0,23.44,58,20,20,0,0,1,29,72.21v3.41c0,
                    5.61,6.52,10.16,14,10.16s14-4.55,14-10.16v-3.4a19.94,
                    19.94,0,0,1,5.52-14.16A26.78,26.78,0,0,0,70.08,39.06Z" />
  </Svg>
}
```

The added benefit of this approach is that every attribute can be edited and animated
using the rest of the React Native ecosystem. In some cases this kind of effort makes a
lot of sense; for example, if you want a vector image to change based on user interaction.

Converting it to a font

If you plan on using the vector in multiple colors and it doesn't contain any color
details, consider making a custom font. IcoMoon (*https://icomoon.io/*) makes it easy
to turn your vector art into a single font (Figure 3-3).

Figure 3-3. The IcoMoon website makes it easy to build a custom font from SVGs

This approach harkens to the *Wyndings* font developed by Microsoft decades ago and
uses the font file format to represent vector images.

The `react-native-vector-icons` (*http://bit.ly/2FUwKUK*) library provides a set of font wrapper functions in addition to commonly used icon sets like FontAwesome, MaterialIcons, and Ionicons.

Install it like any other React Native package via NPM:

```
$> npm install react-native-vector-icons --save
$> react-native link
```

A folder will be created in *android/app/src/main/assets/fonts* for Android as shown in Figure 3-4.

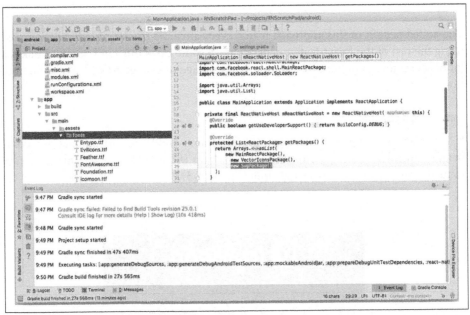

Figure 3-4. Android Studio requires a copy of the font

The linker should also add a *Resources* folder to your iOS project file that contains the set of free fonts. I suggest making sure that the free fonts provided are rendering correctly in your application before loading any custom fonts.

To add an icon set you've downloaded from IcoMoon, you will need two files from the ZIP file provided by IcoMoon: *selection.json* and *icomoon.ttf*. The IcoMoon package will compile all your vector images into different character keys of a font.

For iOS, you will then need to reference the *icomoon.ttf* file in the *Resources* folder and include it as part of the list of *Fonts provided by application* in the *info.plist* as shown in Figure 3-5. For Android, copy the *icomoon.ttf* file to the *android/app/src/main/assets/fonts* folder.

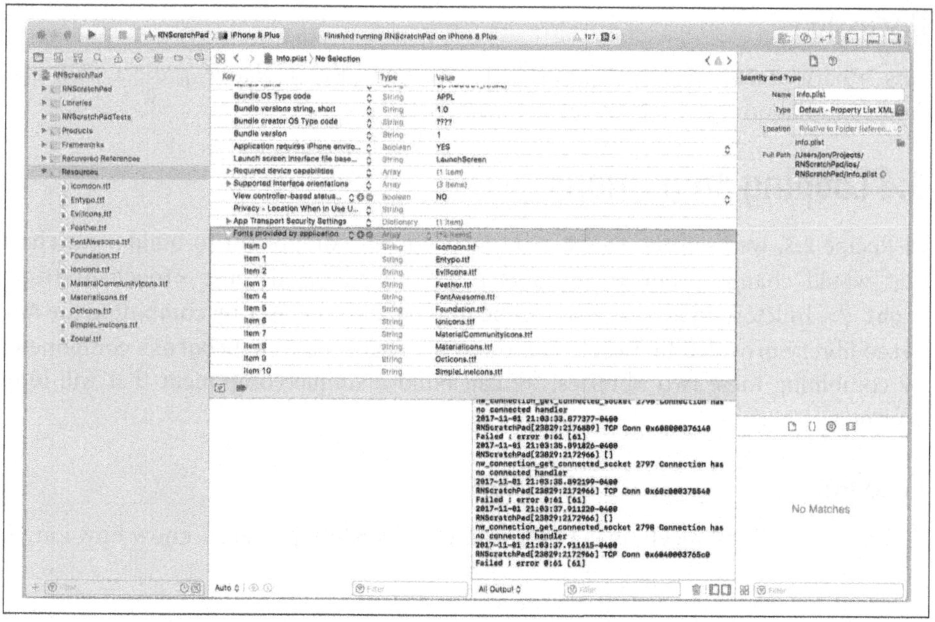

Figure 3-5. Configure Xcode to reference icomoon.ttf

You can now reference the component by icon name. Following is an example of using the *icomoon.ttf* file with an icon called `webinar` next to a FontAwesome icon called `rocket`:

```
import FontAwesomeIcon from 'react-native-vector-icons/FontAwesome';

// Custom IcoMoon Icon
import { createIconSetFromIcoMoon } from 'react-native-vector-icons';
import icoMoonConfig from './fonts/selection.json';
const Icon = createIconSetFromIcoMoon(icoMoonConfig);


export default class App extends Component<{}> {
  render() {
    return (
        <View style={{{flex: 1, justifyContent: 'center', alignItems: 'center' }}>
        <Icon name='webinar' size={30} color='#F00' />
        <FontAwesomeIcon name='rocket' size={30} color='#333' />
      </View>
    );
  }
}
```

Discussion

Any binary assets need to be bundled with your React Native project. iOS and Android will both need references to those assets.

3.4 Looping Animations

In Recipe 2.2, we used the `react-native-progress` component to build a pie chart that would change progress amounts based on a user tapping `<TouchableHighlight />`. Indeterminate progress can be presented to the user by combining the `Animated` library provided by React Native and the `react-native-progress` component. By combining these two libraries, we can build a simple component that will loop forever.

Problem

How do you communicate that a task is in process when you don't know how long it will take?

Solution

Indeterminate progress indicators help you buy time while your application finishes loading. Let's start by defining a constructor with a local state variable in the *components/loading.js* file:

```
constructor(props) {
  super(props);
  this.state = {
    loop: new Animated.Value(0),
  };
}
```

The `loop` variable will refer to an instance of `Animated.Value` that increments from 0 to 1.

`componentDidMount()` is a special function React will call before it renders a component for the first time. We will use this hook into the render loop to configure our loop:

```
componentDidMount() {
  Animated.loop(
    Animated.timing(this.state.loop, {
      toValue: 1,
      duration: 500,
    }),
  ).start();
}
```

Finally we will set up an *interpolation* function so that a corresponding rotation degree results from every value of this.state.loop between 0 and 1. We do not have a direct reference to the animation loop because all interpolation is happening within native components that we are configuring. This approach ensures smooth animations across platforms.

The render() function relies on react-native-progress first presented in Recipe 2.2:

```
render() {
  const interpolation = this.state.loop.interpolate({
    inputRange: [0, 1],
    outputRange: ['0deg', '360deg']
  })
  const animationStyle = {
    transform: [ { rotate: interpolation }  ]
  }
  return <View>
    <Animated.View style={animationStyle}>
      <Pie borderWidth={2} progress={0.2} size={100} color='#2224FF' />
    </Animated.View>
  </View>
}
```

The completed <Loading /> component looks like this:

```
import React, { Component } from 'react';
import {
  Animated,
  View
} from 'react-native';

import Progress, { Pie } from 'react-native-progress';

export default class Loading extends Component {
  constructor(props) {
    super(props);
    this.state = {
      loop: new Animated.Value(0),
    };
  }

  componentDidMount() {
    Animated.loop(
      Animated.timing(this.state.loop, {
        toValue: 1,
        duration: 500,
      }),
    ).start();
  }

  render() {
```

```
      const interpolation = this.state.loop.interpolate({
        inputRange: [0, 1],
        outputRange: ['0deg', '360deg']
      })
      const animationStyle = {
        transform: [ { rotate: interpolation }  ]
      }
      return <View>
        <Animated.View style={animationStyle}>
          <Pie borderWidth={2} progress={0.2} size={100} color='#2224FF' />
        </Animated.View>
      </View>
    }
  }
```

Discussion

In this example, you will notice that the animation is applied to an
<Animated.View /> component instead of a regular <View /> component. These
components are designed to accept values from either an interpolation or an Anima
ted.Value component. This approach avoids calling on the React.js render pipeline,
which would increase the overhead required to render a single frame of the animation.

You should be able to include the <Loading /> component in your application and
watch a spinning pie animation.

See Also

The React Native documentation provides an extensive guide explaining some of the
design choices. There are also plenty of examples.

See the React Native Animation Guide (*http://bit.ly/2FSTsfW*).

CHAPTER 4

Managing Hardware Platforms

You want the best experience for your users. With a mobile device packed with sensors, why not tap into the raw power of the machine running your code to deliver the best possible interaction? With a little bit of work, you can take advantage of the accelerometer, the GPS, the camera, and the hardware on the device. This chapter will survey some of the more common use cases and lessons learned managing the underlying hardware platform.

4.1 Asking for Permission to Use Device Hardware (iOS)

Whether you are snapping photos for a social media app or scanning a QR code in a corporate lobby, the device's camera is one of the most powerful sensors at your disposal.

In some cases, a card or a modal screen with a button that triggers the hardware will help someone understand why they need to provide access like the two-step wireframe depicted in Figure 4-1. This permission flow is common in iOS applications, where permission requests can be delayed until they are required by the application.

Hardware Requires Hardware

The simulator can do some hardware testing; however, especially when dealing with camera data, there is no substitute for a real device.

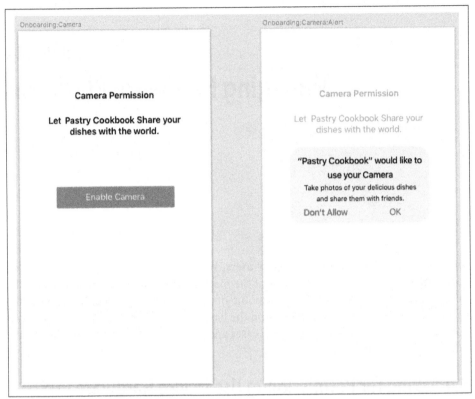

Figure 4-1. A wireframe depicting a two-step user flow for requesting camera permissions

The Apple App Store will review your application and flag any permissions that have not been explicitly declared. In some cases, such as with HealthKit, making background web requests, or using the location information when the app is not active, there may be some other capabilities that will also need to be enabled.

Variations Emerge Closer to the Metal

Most examples in this book assume cross-platform support. Some components, like `react-native-camera`, try (successfully) to abstract the implementation differences between Android and iOS. In some cases, such as Apple Pay or HealthKit, this will not be possible. You will probably end up having to write two implementations in React Native or writing your own React Native bridge.

Problem

How do you design an interface that provides informed consent for users? Ideally, you want to delay requesting permission for hardware until you absolutely need it. In this example, we provide context ensuring that the user gives you access to her camera.

Solution

Let's use the `react-native-camera` component (*http://bit.ly/2C2DM7s*). Another library, `react-native-permissions` (*http://bit.ly/2nJ3ZDI*), will provide us with a standard API for seeing whether we can start using the camera. Begin by installing it from the command line:

```
$> npm install react-native-camera --save
$> npm install react-native-permissions --save
$> react-native link
```

Now add a description under "Privacy - Camera Usage Description" in the *Info.plist* file in Xcode as shown in Figure 4-2.

Figure 4-2. The Info.plist lists your hardware requirements

Create your own `<SimpleCamera />` component that will wrap some basic functionality:

```
// modalCamera.js
import React, { Component } from 'react';
import {
  StyleSheet,
  Text,
  Image,
  View,
  TextInput,
  TouchableHighlight
} from 'react-native'
```

```
import Camera from 'react-native-camera';

export default class ModalCamera extends Component {
  constructor(props) {
    super(props)
    this.state = {
      cameraType: Camera.constants.Type.back
    }
  }

  async capturePhoto() {
    const data = await this.camera.capture();
    this.props.onPhoto(data);
  }

  switchCamera = () => {
    const { Type } = Camera.constants;
    const cameraType = this.state.cameraType === Type.back ?
    Type.front : Type.back;
    this.setState({ cameraType });
  }

  takePicture = () => {
    this.capturePhoto();
  }


  render() {
    return <View style={{flex: 1, backgroundColor: 'blue' }}>
      <Camera
          ref={(cam) => { this.camera = cam; }}
          aspect={Camera.constants.Aspect.fill}
          captureTarget={Camera.constants.CaptureTarget.disk}
          captureAudio={false}
          style={styles.container}
          type={this.state.cameraType}>
          <View style={styles.buttonRow}>
            <TouchableHighlight style={styles.button}
            onPress={this.switchCamera}>
              <Text style={styles.buttonText}>Switch</Text>
            </TouchableHighlight>
            <TouchableHighlight style={styles.button}
            onPress={this.takePicture}>
              <Text style={styles.buttonText}>Snap Dish</Text>
            </TouchableHighlight>
          </View>
        </Camera>
      </View>
  }
}

const styles = StyleSheet.create({
```

```
    container: {
      flex: 1,
      backgroundColor: "transparent",
    },
    buttonRow: {
      flexDirection: "row",
      position: 'absolute',
      bottom: 25,
      right: 0,
      left: 0,
      justifyContent: "center"
    },
    button: {
      padding: 20,
      borderWidth: 3,
      borderColor: "#FF0000",
      margin: 15
    },
    buttonText: {
      color: "#FFF",
      fontWeight: 'bold'
    },
})
```

The *App.js* file will highlight some of the potential states for the camera hardware on the device. By using `react-native-permissions`, we can create a user experience where someone is alerted only when the camera request needs to be made. This library also claims to support the latest Android permission checks:

```
// App.js
import React, { Component } from 'react';
import {
  Alert,
  StyleSheet,
  TouchableHighlight,
  View,
  Text
} from 'react-native'
import SimpleCamera from './simpleCamera'
import Permissions from 'react-native-permissions'
export default class App extends Component {

  constructor(props) {
    super(props);
    this.state = { cameraPermission: null };
  }

  componentDidMount() {
    this.determinePermission();
  }

  async determinePermission(){
```

```
    const cameraPermission = await Permissions.check('camera')
    this.setState({ cameraPermission });
  }

  async requestCamera() {
    const cameraPermission = await Permissions.request('camera');
    this.setState({ cameraPermission });
  }

  photoTaken = ({ path }) => {
    Alert.alert(`Photo Path: ${path}`)
  }

  requestPermission = () => {
    this.requestCamera();
  }

  renderDenied() {
    return <View>
      <Text style={styles.textHeading}>Looks like you do not want
      to take any photos.</Text>
      <Text style={styles.textHeading}>
        Please enable camera functionality in your application settings
      </Text>
    </View>
  }

  renderCameraRequest() {
    return <View>
      <Text style={styles.textHeading}>
        Let Pastry Cookbook share your dishes with the world!
      </Text>
      <TouchableHighlight style={styles.button}
      onPress={this.requestPermission}>
        <Text style={styles.buttonText}>Enable Camera</Text>
      </TouchableHighlight>
    </View>
  }


  render() {
    const { cameraPermission } = this.state;
    return <View style={styles.container}>
      { cameraPermission === "undetermined" && this.renderCameraRequest() }
      { cameraPermission === "authorized" && <SimpleCamera
      onPhoto={this.photoTaken} /> }
      { cameraPermission === "denied" && this.renderDenied() }
    </View>
  }
}

const styles = StyleSheet.create({
```

```
  container: {
    flex: 1,
    paddingTop: 30,
    backgroundColor: '#000',
  },
  buttonRow: {
    flexDirection: 'row',
    position: 'absolute',
    bottom: 25,
    right: 0,
    left: 0,
    justifyContent: 'center'
  },
  button: {
    padding: 20,
    borderWidth: 3,
    borderColor: '#FFF',
    borderRadius: 20,
    backgroundColor: '#2445A2',
    margin: 15
  },
  buttonText: {
    color: '#FFF',
    fontWeight: 'bold',
    textAlign: 'center',
  },
  textHeading: {
    color: '#44CAE5' ,
    fontSize: 24,
    padding: 20,
    fontWeight: 'bold',
    textAlign: 'center',

  }
})
```

You can see the different application states in Figure 4-3 and Figure 4-4. When a screenshot is taken, an `Alert` presents the user with the filepath on the device. In Recipe 4.4 we will explore the filesystem in more depth.

Using Async/Await Instead of Promise()

Working with device hardware is rarely synchronous. In other words, the user interface will not block to wait until data from a sensor returns correctly. The result of this asynchronicity is often seen in a series of nested then(() => {}) statements. In order to get around this, I've decided to present this example using `async` and `await`. If you feel more comfortable with chaining then() instead, the examples should work just the same.

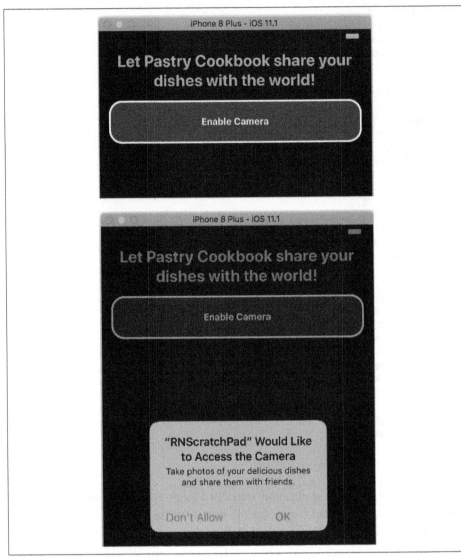

Figure 4-3. Delaying hardware device permissions provides users with a better user experience

Figure 4-4. Handling a case when you don't have permission to use the camera is critical; with permission granted, photoTaken() presents an Alert with the file path of the photo taken

See Also

This example only scratches the surface of requesting permission from users. If your application will play music in the background, enable payments, track users, or anything that can be deemed invasive, expect to spend development time informing users.

Learn more about requesting permissions from the react-native-permissions GitHub page (*http://bit.ly/2nJ3ZDI*) and the PermissionsAndroid React Native guide (*http://bit.ly/2EN3H61*).

4.2 Fetching Paginated Requests

The infinite scroll is an endless feast of content. Just as your palette is about to surrender, you find yourself faced with a new batch of morsels to tempt further consumption.

Most applications rely on the networking infrastructure on the mobile device to make asynchronous calls to a web server, oftentimes to get a list of records. This interaction pattern is seen in most applications that present a list of choices to a user. Whether it's a series of photos from people you follow, or the latest restaurant choices in your area, an ever-growing list of content keeps people engaged.

Problem

How do you present a paginated list of content that can be constantly refreshed?

Solution

Before we tackle the pagination challenge, we need a data provider that we can connect to. Building a web server falls outside the scope of this book, so we will rely on the *JSONPlaceholder* (*https://jsonplaceholder.typicode.com*), a REST API for prototyping and testing, instead of rolling our own.

See the `FlatList` in Figure 4-5, which renders a paginated set of results.

This example relies on two components as shown in Figure 4-5: `<ListItem />` and the container `<App />`.

Figure 4-5. A FlatList renders a paginated result set

The `<ListItem />` is just a simple function that returns JSX. The overlay effect is achieved by relying on absolute positioning of the `{title}` and a backing `<View />`, which is semitransparent. The React Native guides recommend always passing `height` and `width` information for dynamic images. In this case, we're relying on a third-party web service called *LoremPixel*, and we can dictate what format we require:

```
//listItem.js
import React, { Component } from 'react';

import {
```

```
    Image,
    StyleSheet,
    View,
    Text
} from 'react-native';


export default function ({url, title, width}) {
  return <View style={styles.card}>
    <Image resizeMode='cover'
      source={ { uri: url  } }
      style={[styles.image, {width, height: 200}] } />
    <View style={[styles.overlay, { width }]} />
    <Text style={styles.text}>{title}</Text>
  </View>
}

const styles = StyleSheet.create({
  card: {
    borderBottomWidth: 5,
    borderTopWidth: 2,
    borderBottomColor: '#222',
    borderTopColor: '#CACACA',
    borderStyle: 'solid',
    height: 207,
  },

  overlay: {...StyleSheet.absoluteFillObject,
    height: 30,
    top: 170,
    position: 'absolute',
    backgroundColor: 'rgba(2,2,2,0.8)',

  },

  text: {
    fontSize: 14,
    height: 30,
    top: 170,
    color: '#FFF',
    backgroundColor: 'transparent',
  },

  image: {...StyleSheet.absoluteFillObject, }
});
```

This component illustrates the critical relationship between `<RefreshControl />` and `<FlatList />`. The `fetchRecords()` method asynchrously fetches JSON results and appends them to `this.state.list`. `fetchRecords()` is called on first load, `compo nentDidMount()`, when a refresh happens from a *Pull to Refresh* event and when the user scrolls to the bottom of the list. `appendResults()` copies the retrieved list of posts into a new array with the existing list after performing a small set of transformations.

 In order for iOS to make a web request, the URL must either use SSL (begin with https) or the domain must be explicitly set as exempt in the *Info.plist* file under NSExceptionDomains. This may be required if you are running a web development server locally without SSL.

```
//App.js
import React, { Component } from 'react';
import {
  StyleSheet,
  FlatList,
  Dimensions,
  RefreshControl,
  View,
  Text
} from 'react-native';

import ListItem from './listItem'

const { width } = Dimensions.get('window');
const API = 'https://jsonplaceholder.typicode.com';

export default class App extends Component<{}> {

  constructor(props) {
    super(props)
    this.state = {
      refreshing: false,
      page: 1,
      list: []
    }
  }

  resultToListItem({ id, title }) {
    const { page } = this.state;
    const url = `https://lorempixel.com/${width}/200/food/${title}/`
    return { id: `${page}-${id}`, title: `${page} - ${title}`, width, url }
  }

  appendResults(results) {
    let list = [];
    Object.keys(results).forEach( (photoKey) => {
      list.push(this.resultToListItem(results[photoKey]));
    });
    this.setState( (prevState) => ({
      list: prevState.list.concat(list),
      refreshing: false,
```

```
      page: (prevState.page + 1)
    }));
  }

  async fetchRecords() {
    this.setState({ refreshing: true });
    const resp = await fetch(`${API}/posts?_limit=5`)
    const results = await resp.json();
    this.appendResults(results);
  }

  onRefresh = () => {
    this.setState({ list: [], page: 1 });
    this.fetchRecords();
  }

  onEndReached = () => {
    this.fetchRecords()
  }

  componentDidMount() {
    this.fetchRecords()
  }

  render() {
    const refreshControl = <RefreshControl refreshing={this.state.refreshing}
      onRefresh={this.onRefresh} />
    return <View style={styles.container}>
      <View style={styles.header}>
      { this.state.refreshing ?
      <Text style={styles.headerText}>Refreshing...</Text> :
          <Text style={styles.headerText}>
          {this.state.list.length} Meals
          </Text> }
      </View>
      <FlatList
        renderItem={({item}) => <ListItem {...item} />}
        refreshControl={refreshControl}
        keyExtractor={({id}) => id}
        data={this.state.list}
        onEndReached={this.onEndReached}
      />
    </View>
  }
}

const styles = StyleSheet.create({
  container: {
    flex: 1,
    paddingTop: 30,
    backgroundColor: '#FFF',
  },
```

```
headerText: {
  color: '#144595',
  fontSize: 16,
  fontWeight: 'bold',
  textAlign: 'center',
},

header: {
  borderBottomWidth: 1,
  borderBottomColor: '#222',
  borderStyle: "solid",
}
})
```

Discussion

Implementing this pattern requires a little bit of care. Because the user can trigger a refresh at any point, and because the list of content is expanding, it's best to use some native data structures for handling the content. Furthermore, the server may return the same content twice, making it necessary to handle duplicates. Page sizes may also vary and so the resulting list on the client might be a mash of slightly different queries to an API.

See Also

For lists that have a section that sticks to the top of the view, consider using the Sec tionList (*http://bit.ly/2E8S88i*). The API is very similar.

Managing records inside of a component can also lead to some confusion. For example, if you wanted to tap into one of these records to retrieve further information or perform a route navigation (see Recipe 2.4), then some global state management with Flux, Mobx, Redux, Apollo, or Relay may be worth considering.

4.3 Save Application State with Redux and Local Storage

Redux is one of the most popular state management libraries in the React ecosystem. Unidirectional data flow architectures like Flux, Mobx, and Redux go with React like peanut butter and strawberry jam. But what happens when a user closes your app, taps a notification, or shifts the application from a foreground state to a background state? How do we ensure that data persists in these cases?

There are many strategies for persisting data on mobile. Each app has access to some file storage; however, for data, the *AsyncStorage* module provides a simple API for keeping track of important information.

This example combines one of the most popular state management libraries (Redux) with the most commonly used persistence module in React Native: AsyncStorage.

Problem

You are already using Redux and have decided to adopt it for your mobile application. You noticed that users like to have data cached locally even after they have closed the application.

Solution

The redux-persist library is an excellent starting point in resolving this issue. This NPM mobile was conceived with support from AsyncStorage. As your Redux architecture grows, some of the most recent design changes in version 5.x of redux-persist will come in handy. This example relies on the project started in Recipe 2.5, but any Redux application should work.

In our case, we begin by installing redux-persist:

```
$> npm i redux-persist --save
```

By adjusting the *src/appContainer.js* and the *reduxStore.js* files from Recipe 2.5, our appication will automatically store the username and application state in asynchronous storage.

reduxStore.js used to rely on the combineReducers() method. This has been replaced with persistCombineReducers(), which includes a config parameter. storage will automatically resolve to AsyncStorage with React Native:

```
// reduxStore.js
import * as reducers from './src/reducers';
import { createStore, applyMiddleware, combineReducers, compose} from 'redux';
import { persistCombineReducers } from 'redux-persist';
import storage from 'redux-persist/es/storage';
import logger from 'redux-logger';
const config = {
  key: 'root',
  storage,
};
export default createStore(
  combineReducers(reducers),
  persistCombineReducers(config, reducers),
  applyMiddleware(logger)
);
```

redux-persist includes a <PersistGate /> component, which is intended to limit rendering of your application until the application state has been completely hydrated:

```
// src/appContainer.js
import React, { Component } from 'react';
import AppContainer from './src/appContainer';
import { Provider } from 'react-redux';
import store from './reduxStore';

// newly-added references to redux-persist:
import { persistStore } from 'redux-persist';
import { PersistGate } from 'redux-persist/es/integration/react';
const persistor = persistStore(store);

export default class App extends Component<{}> {

  render() {
    return <Provider store={store}>
      <PersistGate persistor={persistor}>
        <AppContainer />
      </PersistGate>
    </Provider>
  }
}
```

When the app is terminated and restarted, any state changes should be maintained in AsyncStorage. `redux-persist` is an excellent example of how the Redux design philosophy enables plugging in libraries by extending the core Redux architecture based on your application's use case.

See Also

As your app grows, you will undoubtedly want to selectively persist portions of your application. `redux-persist` provides mechanisms for handling state changes, whitelisting, and blacklisting of reducers and parameters. Consult the documentation for more information (*http://bit.ly/2nPdsst*). Another excellent library is `redux-offline` (*http://bit.ly/2Ealnrl*), which depends on `redux-persist` and provides additional hooks for handling poor network connectivity scenarios.

4.4 Using the Filesystem

There are a lot of common use cases for working with an application's filesystem: dealing with binary files, downloading assets from the web, or like in Recipe 4.1, because you want to manage photos inside your app.

We're going to extend the project started in Recipe 4.1 by adding listing, viewing, and deleting functionality to the same application with the `react-native-fs` package.

Problem

How do you tackle some of the common challenges when dealing with the filesystem, such as how to write, delete, list, and view files?

Solution

Our solution involves refactoring *App.js* from Recipe 4.1 into a `<CameraContainer />` component. Our updated *App.js* file can toggle between a *camera view* (*cameraContainer.js*) and a *list view* (*listContainer.js*). Figure 4-6 demonstrates the addition of a button group for toggling pages in the *App.js* file.

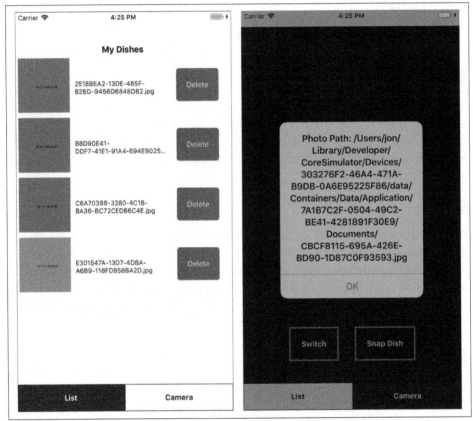

Figure 4-6. The App.js now includes a bottom toggle for page switching; CameraContainer and ListContainer are loaded interchangeably

Begin by installing the `react-native-fs` package (*http://bit.ly/2E9SMqg*):

```
$> npm install react-native-fs --save
$> react-native link react-native-fs
```

Let's move the existing *App.js* file to a new *cameraContainer.js* file:

```
// cameraContainer.js
import React, { Component } from 'react';
import {
  Alert,
  StyleSheet,
  TouchableHighlight,
  View,
  Text
} from 'react-native';

import SimpleCamera from './simpleCamera';
import Permissions from 'react-native-permissions';

export default class CameraContainer extends Component<{}> {

  constructor(props) {
    super(props);
    this.state = { cameraPermission: null };
  }

  componentDidMount() {
    this.determinePermission();
  }

  async determinePermission(){
    const cameraPermission = await Permissions.check('camera')
    this.setState({ cameraPermission });
  }

  async requestCamera() {
    const cameraPermission = await Permissions.request('camera');
    this.setState({ cameraPermission });
  }

  photoTaken = ({ path }) => {
    Alert.alert(`Photo Path: ${path}`)
  }

  requestPermission = () => {
    this.requestCamera();
  }

  renderDenied() {
    return <View>
      <Text style={styles.textHeading}>Looks like you do not want to
      take any photos.</Text>
      <Text style={styles.textHeading}>
        Please enable camera functionality in your application settings
      </Text>
    </View>
  }
```

```
  renderCameraRequest() {
    return <View>
      <Text style={styles.textHeading}>
        Let Pastry Cookbook share your dishes with the world!
      </Text>
      <TouchableHighlight style={styles.button} onPress={this.requestPermission}>
        <Text style={styles.buttonText}>Enable Camera</Text>
      </TouchableHighlight>
    </View>
  }


  render() {
    const { cameraPermission } = this.state;
    return <View style={styles.container}>
      { cameraPermission === "undetermined" && this.renderCameraRequest() }
      { cameraPermission === "authorized" && <SimpleCamera
          onPhoto={this.photoTaken} /> }
      { cameraPermission === "denied" && this.renderDenied() }
    </View>
  }
}

const styles = StyleSheet.create({
  container: {
    flex: 1,
    paddingTop: 30,
    backgroundColor: '#000',
  },
  buttonRow: {
    flexDirection: 'row',
    position: 'absolute',
    bottom: 25,
    right: 0,
    left: 0,
    justifyContent: 'center'
  },
  button: {
    padding: 20,
    borderWidth: 3,
    borderColor: '#FFF',
    borderRadius: 20,
    backgroundColor: '#2445A2',
    margin: 15
  },
  buttonText: {
    color: '#FFF',
    fontWeight: 'bold',
    textAlign: 'center',
  },
  textHeading: {
```

```
    color: '#44CAE5',
    fontSize: 24,
    padding: 20,
    fontWeight: 'bold',
    textAlign: 'center',

  }
});
```

App.js will now set the page state between the list and camera states:

```
// App.js
import React, { Component } from 'react';
import {
  StyleSheet,
  TouchableHighlight,
  View,
  Text
} from 'react-native';
import CameraContainer from './cameraContainer';
import ListContainer from './listContainer';
export default class App extends Component<{}> {
  constructor(props) {
    super(props);
    this.state = {
      page: "list"
    }
  }

  render() {
    const { page } = this.state;
    return <View style={styles.container}>
      { page === "list" && <ListContainer style={styles.page} /> }
      { page === "camera" && <CameraContainer style={styles.page} /> }
      <View style={styles.buttonGroup}>
        <TouchableHighlight
          onPress={ () => { this.setState( { page: 'list' } ) } }
          style={[styles.button, (page === "list" &&
          styles.activeButton) ]} >
            <Text style={[styles.buttonText, (page === "list" &&
            styles.activeButtonText) ]}>
              List
            </Text>
        </TouchableHighlight>
        <TouchableHighlight
          onPress={ () => { this.setState( { page: 'camera' } ) } }
          style={[styles.button, (page === "camera" && styles.activeButton) ]} >
          <Text style={[styles.buttonText,
          (page === "camera" && styles.activeButtonText) ]}>
            Camera
          </Text>
        </TouchableHighlight>
      </View>
```

```
        </View>
      }
    }

const styles = StyleSheet.create({
  container: {
    flex: 1,
    paddingTop: 30,
    backgroundColor: '#FFF',
  },
  page: {
    flex: 1,
  },
  buttonGroup: {
    flexDirection: 'row',
  },
  activeButton: {
    backgroundColor: '#343678',
  },
  activeButtonText: {
    color: '#FFF'
  },
  button: {
    borderWidth: 1,
    borderColor: '#242668',
    flex: 1,
    height: 50,
    justifyContent: 'center',
  },
  buttonText: {
    fontWeight: 'bold',
    textAlign: 'center',
    color: '#242668',
  }
});
```

The new `<ListContainer />` component will begin by scanning the documents directory and populating a local `this.state` variable on `componentDidMount()`:

```
// listContainer.js
import React, { Component } from 'react';
import {
  FlatList,
  StyleSheet,
  Image,
  TouchableHighlight,
  View,
  Text
} from 'react-native';

import {
  unlink,
  readDir,
```

```
    DocumentDirectoryPath
  } from 'react-native-fs';

  export default class ListContainer extends Component<{}> {

    constructor(props) {
      super(props);
      this.state = { photos: [] }
    }

    componentDidMount() {
      this.refreshPhotoList();
    }

    async deletePhoto(path){
      await unlink(path)
      this.refreshPhotoList();
    }

    async refreshPhotoList() {
      const allFiles = await readDir(DocumentDirectoryPath);
      const photos = allFiles.filter( (file) =>
      { return file.path.split('.')[1] === "jpg" })
      this.setState({ photos });
    }

    renderRow(file) {
      return <View style={styles.row}>
        <Image style={{width: 100, height: 100}} resizeMode='cover'
        source={{ uri: file.path }} />
        <Text numberOfLines={2}
          style={styles.rowText} >{file.name}</Text>
        <TouchableHighlight style={styles.deleteButton}
          onPress={() => this.deletePhoto(file.path)}>
          <Text style={styles.deleteButtonText} >Delete</Text>
        </TouchableHighlight>
      </View>
    }

    render() {
      return <View style={styles.container}>
        <Text style={styles.titleText}>My Dishes</Text>
        <FlatList
          keyExtractor={ ({ name }) => name }
          data={this.state.photos}
          renderItem={ ({ item }) => this.renderRow(item) }
          />
      </View>
    }
  };

  const styles = StyleSheet.create({
```

```
      container: {
        flex: 1,
        paddingTop: 30,
        backgroundColor: '#FFF',
      },
      row: {
        flexDirection: 'row',
        margin: 5,
      },
      rowText: {
        fontSize: 12,
        flex: 1,
        paddingLeft: 10,
        paddingTop: 40
      },
      titleText: {
        fontSize: 16,
        textAlign: 'center',
        fontWeight: 'bold',
        height: 20,
      },
      deleteButton: {
        backgroundColor: '#A22',
        justifyContent: 'center',
        margin: 20,
        width: 80,
        borderRadius: 5,
      },
      deleteButtonText: {
        color: '#FFF',
        textAlign: 'center',
        justifyContent: 'center',
      }
    });
```

We render the photos using a `<FlatList />` component (discussed further in Recipe
4.2). Notice that `refreshPhotoList` is called asynchronously: all calls to the filesystem are blocking calls and therefore do not happen synchronously. By relying on
React's `this.state` variable, we can trigger a render on `setState()`, whenever it happens next. `DocumentDirectoryPath` is a global variable that `react-native-fs`
resolves based on the platform and the application. Any absolute path manipulations
(such as reading a directory with `readDir`) will require using this constant.

See Also

This example only scratches the surface of what's possible. Use `react-native-fs` in
combination with `react-native-zip-archive` (*http://bit.ly/2C3c8Hp*) to ZIP files
before sending them. `react-native-fs` can also provide large data storage with

redux-persist on the Android platform thanks to projects like redux-persist-filesystem-storage (*http://bit.ly/2Em78Df*).

CHAPTER 5

Lift Off! Sharing Your App

If you are just beginning to deploy native applications, plan for unexpected delays! For example, the deployment process with the Apple App Store requires several administrative hurdles that fall outside the scope of this cookbook, but are worth keeping in mind. Expect to deploy several iterations of your app before it's ready for primetime.

Navigating each platform marketplace means acquainting yourself with new terminology and user interface particularities. The sections that follow include some tools and lessons learned for making this process as smooth as possible. I will also walk you through the testing model with the Apple App Store and then finish the chapter with some tips for dealing with platform-specific code that might surface as you deal with cross-platform delivery.

5.1 Automate Publishing Your App

You find yourself clicking through the Apple and Google stores over and over again to get through to beta or production. These user interfaces are error prone and mean that you can't keep your store description in lock step with your app.

Problem

How can we keep as much of our App Store configuration versioned like any other source code if we want to send our build to a *continuous integration* service like bitrise (*https://www.bitrise.io/*)? The answer is scripting our deployments. My personal favorite is *fastlane* (*https://fastlane.tools/*).

Solution

fastlane is a powerful tool for simplifying the deployment of your application to the Google Play Store and the Apple App Store. At its core, fastlane is a collection of little tools that each do one thing well. They are written in Ruby, so you will need to have a recent version installed.

fastlane is a *rubygem*. This is akin to a *package* in NPM. Installing Ruby will be slightly different depending on your operating system. The Ruby Language download page (*https://www.ruby-lang.org/en/downloads/*) includes instructions for all major operating systems. If you are a software developer using macOS, you will likely already be using Homebrew (*https://brew.sh/*) to install open source software easily.

Installing Ruby with Homebrew is as simple as:

```
$> brew install ruby
$> sudo gem install fastlane
```

The sudo command is required to install rubygems globally. You will be prompted to provide your system password to complete the installation. You should now be able to navigate to your project folder and type fastlane on the command line.

Setting up fastlane

fastlane recommends having a separate *fastlane/* folder for both iOS and Android. Because React Native applications have a project root folder, I recommend centralizing all your fastlane configuration in a *fastlane/* folder at the root of your project.

 Semantic versioning (also called semver (*http://semver.org/*)) is the widely practiced decision to use two points and three ordinals to denote the <major>.<minor>.<patch> version of an artifact. By default, Android Studio and Xcode will not set up this versioning structure for your application. Change it if you want fastlane to be able to automatically increment your build numbers.

If you decide to put a *fastlane/* folder inside the *android/* and *ios/* folders, respectively, you can follow the steps in the command-line wizard:

```
$> cd ios/ # or android
$> fastlane
Could not find fastlane in current directory. Make sure to have your fastlane
configuration files inside a folder called "fastlane". Would you like to set
fastlane up? (y/n)
```

From there fastlane will detect what sort of project it is and create a Fastfile. The Fastfile will define different *lanes*: different deployment-related tasks, such as running a test suite, deploying to private beta, or publishing to a public audience.

Almost all the metadata fields (such as contact information, company name, demo account details, etc.) will be the same across platforms. Reduce copy/paste errors by storing these details in the appropriate file structure. For one project, my *fastlane/* files are set up to handle the beta deployment on Android and iOS by simply running `fastlane android beta` or `fastlane ios beta` from the project root folder.

Here's a sample *fastlane/* folder structure that includes an en-CA localization:

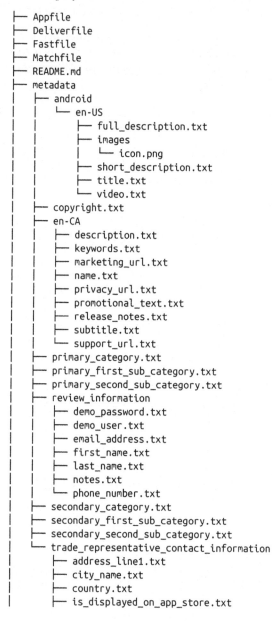

```
├── Appfile
├── Deliverfile
├── Fastfile
├── Matchfile
├── README.md
├── metadata
│   ├── android
│   │   └── en-US
│   │       ├── full_description.txt
│   │       ├── images
│   │       │   └── icon.png
│   │       ├── short_description.txt
│   │       ├── title.txt
│   │       └── video.txt
│   ├── copyright.txt
│   ├── en-CA
│   │   ├── description.txt
│   │   ├── keywords.txt
│   │   ├── marketing_url.txt
│   │   ├── name.txt
│   │   ├── privacy_url.txt
│   │   ├── promotional_text.txt
│   │   ├── release_notes.txt
│   │   ├── subtitle.txt
│   │   └── support_url.txt
│   ├── primary_category.txt
│   ├── primary_first_sub_category.txt
│   ├── primary_second_sub_category.txt
│   ├── review_information
│   │   ├── demo_password.txt
│   │   ├── demo_user.txt
│   │   ├── email_address.txt
│   │   ├── first_name.txt
│   │   ├── last_name.txt
│   │   ├── notes.txt
│   │   └── phone_number.txt
│   ├── secondary_category.txt
│   ├── secondary_first_sub_category.txt
│   ├── secondary_second_sub_category.txt
│   └── trade_representative_contact_information
│       ├── address_line1.txt
│       ├── city_name.txt
│       ├── country.txt
│       ├── is_displayed_on_app_store.txt
```

```
|        ├─ postal_code.txt
|        ├─ state.txt
|        └─ trade_name.txt
└─ report.xml
```

Fastfile

fastlane looks for a `Fastfile` that describes the different commands available. When you type `fastlane ios beta`, you are calling the *iOS* platform and the *beta* lane.

Integration with a team chat service like *Slack* can keep everyone informed if a build fails. Consider that fastlane may also be run by a special server designed to do a deployment after code has been merged by a code-hosting platform like GitHub or BitBucket.

This project is called `RNScratchpad` and the `Fastfile` is stored in *RNScratchpad/fastlane/Fastfile*:

```
platform :ios do
  before_all do
    ENV["GYM_PROJECT"] = "ios/RNScratchpad.xcodeproj"
  end

  desc "Submit a beta to Apple TestFlight"
  lane :beta do
    match
    ensure_git_status_clean
    increment_build_number(xcodeproj: "ios/RNScratchpad.xcodeproj")
    gym(scheme: "RNScratchpad", export_xcargs: "-allowProvisioningUpdates")
    testflight
  end

  after_all do |lane|
    # This block is called, only if the executed lane was successful
    send_message_to_slack(
      "Successfully deployed new update",
      "ios",
      true
    )
  end

  error do |lane, exception|
    send_message_to_slack(
      exception.message,
      "ios",
      false
    )
  end
end
```

The :beta lane relies on a collection of functions that are part of the fastlane family. match, ensure_git_status_clean, increment_build_number, gym, and testflight are individual commands that run one after another. In some cases they have their own configuration files.

match relies on a Matchfile. match is a critical piece of tooling for managing iOS provisioning profiles and certificates. If you have multiple team members involved in deploying your application, I recommend following the match setup guide (*http:// bit.ly/2sdXPjD*).

You can run each of the commands individually. For example, you can build your Xcode project with gym by running:

```
$> cd fastlane/
$> fastlane gym
```

ensure_git_status_clean will protect you from making the common mistake of deploying code that has not yet been committed to source control. incre ment_build_number will increase the build number automatically in the *Info.plist*, saving you from the manual step of increasing the number before being able to send your application to Apple. gym will trigger xcodebuild and compile your project. Using gym with a properly defined scheme will ensure that React Native is built for production. Because you are writing a JavaScript bundle, React Native needs to store a *jsbundle* file as part of the compilation process. This only happens in production.

Further down in the file, send_message_to_slack() is defined. Notice that the xcode proj: symbol key is provided as a hint to fastlane. The slack_url would of course be specific to your team:

```
def send_message_to_slack(message, platform, success)
  if platform == 'android'
    build_number = get_version_code('android/app')
    version_name = get_version_name('android/app')
  elsif platform == 'ios'
    version = get_version_number(xcodeproj: 'ios/RNScratchpad.xcodeproj')
    build_number = get_build_number(xcodeproj: 'ios/RNScratchpad.xcodeproj')
  end
  slack(
    slack_url: "https://hooks.slack.com/services/TEAM_VAR/KEY/SERVICE",
    message: message,
    attachment_properties: {
      fields: [{
                title: 'Version',
                value: version_name,
                short: true
            },
            {
                title: 'Build Number',
                value: build_number,
```

```
                short: true
            }]
      },
      success: success
    )
  end
```

Defining store metadata

Each file provides one bit of text. For example, *trade_representative_contact_information/city_name.txt* simply includes:

```
Boston
```

Discussion

The first time you deploy your app in each store, you will have to go through an extensive registration process. This includes paying an annual fee, providing legal information, and categorizing your application. Unfortunately, the tools provided are the same whether you are going through them the first time or subsequent times.

See Also

Be patient with yourself when setting up tools like fastlane. They provide a lot of documentation as you move forward, but you should expect to run the build process dozens of times until it works perfectly for your environment and project requirements.

I recommend looking at the Getting Started guides (*https://docs.fastlane.tools/*). Once you've attempted to deliver your project to the Play Store or the App Store, slowly add more and more tools to your fastlane configuration. Look at the fastlane examples project configurations (*https://github.com/fastlane/examples*). The Mattermost mobile application (*http://bit.ly/2GXaRoX*) also has a `Fastfile` configuration that is specific to React Native and worth reviewing.

5.2 Sharing Your iOS App with Beta Testers

Your pile of React components is shaping up to do something you and your users are excited about. While you could ask everyone to install React Native and download the source code to compile for themselves, why not use some of the tools Apple has provided to share your app with the world?

Problem

How does my team test my app? You will probably have a group of friends, colleagues, or investors that want to kick the tires on your new application before it's

---

launched to the broader public. If you want to appear on the Apple App Store, you will need to be acquainted with the different kinds of testers available to you in *Test-Flight*, Apple's beta testing toolkit for iOS.

Solution

iTunes Connect divides application testers into two categories: *Internal Testers* and *External Testers*. Internal Testers must have an iTunes Connect account, meaning that they:

1. Must be invited to join iTunes Connect
2. Must accept the invitation

 If you plan on testing your app on Android, each of your testers will need a Google account (@gmail.com or G Suite) to be included.

Once they are members of your iTunes Connect account, they can then be designated as Internal Testers for your app. They will then be sent another email where they will be invited to download TestFlight—an app-downloading service for beta software.

This multistep process is not simple, but it means that your app can be used without undergoing an Apple review process. External Testers, which can number in the thousands, can receive early builds only after they have undergone an Apple review step. This often requires having demo credentials and making sure that all Apple review guidelines are followed. Expect delays if you are using special app features like HealthKit or tracking location in the background. If your app allows users to share their own content, make sure you have support for flagging inappropriate content in place before the submission process. I would recommend getting any project managers or leadership roles set up as iTunes Connect users early on in the project so that they can see progress on their own personal devices.

Discussion

iTunes Connect is Apple's response to two questions: "How do I test my app with beta testers?" and "How do I put my app on the App Store (and make money)?" There are a few steps to getting onto iTunes Connect: you (or your organization) need to register as Apple Developers. There is a yearly fee, and in the case of organizations, a D-U-N-S number (*http://bit.ly/2nIwLo1*) (a widely used indexing number for entities) is also required. Once you are an Apple Developer, you should be able to visit *https://developer.apple.com*. If your application relies on additional features, such as push notification or the iAd platform, some further configuration will be required. Make sure you have an iCloud account under the Membership section of the platform. Once you have an Apple Developer account, you should be able to log in with this account in Xcode and also have access to iTunes Connect.

See Also

Apple describes the membership details (*https://apple.co/2BJKvrb*) in a fair amount of detail. My experience is that this whole process needs to be done a few times before it begins to click.

5.3 Configuring Application Settings

React Native enables easy cross-platform and cross-device development. You will already have at least a development environment and a production environment for your application. If you support tablet and phone, Android and iOS, and a development and production environment, then you have eight possible configurations for your application.

There are a number of tools for assisting in the complexities of multidevice (iOS/Android) and multienvironment (production/development) software. In Recipe 1.3, I touched on one of the mechanisms at your disposal, a platform suffix in a component. Another useful library is `Platform`, which makes handling platform-specific code easier to manage. The `__DEV__` global constant can be used to determine whether we're in a development or production environment. Lastly, the `react-native-device-info` package is an excellent one-stop shop for learning everything about a device. Let's go through when you might use which tools.

Problem

What are some common challenges facing cross-platform development?

Spacing between views or sizing of typography may be different across platforms. You may find that iOS devices are rendering `padding` and `margin` properties inconsistently. You may also decide that you want to render a different *sidebar* depending on whether the app is running on a tablet or a phone. Finally, your configuration of logging and/or hostnames for servers may be dependent on the environment. For example, you may want the app to connect to `http://localhost:8000` when in development and `https://myapp.com/api` when in production.

Solution

Let's unpack these issues one by one. Start by distinguishing whether you are working with Android or iOS. Next, we will tackle production and development environments. Then we can further tailor our user experience by adjusting how components render on a tablet or a phone.

There are platform-specific styles

In Recipe 3.1 we looked at how you can build a global stylesheet for your application. At the top of the file, you can reference the `Platform` library that comes with `react-native`:

```
// updated styles.js
import { Platform, Dimensions } from 'react-native';
const { width, height } = Dimensions.get('window');
```

While defining your styles, you can now seamlessly tweak the user interface on a per-platform basis. Assume we've defined a default amount of spacing; now we can use these values to tailor our components:

```
const IOS_SPACING = 15;
const ANDROID_SPACING = 20;

// GLOBAL STYLES
export const globalStyles = {
  textHeader: {...fontSizes.H1,
    color: '#2A547A',
    paddingTop: 20,
    fontWeight: 'bold',
  },
  button: {
    backgroundColor: '#2A547A',
    minWidth: 40,
    ...Platform.select({
      android: { paddingTop: ANDROID_SPACING },
      ios: { paddingTop: IOS_SPACING }
    }),
  },
};
```

The resulting `globalStyles.button` will have slightly different padding for iOS and Android.

Android and iOS use different components

Sometimes a component used on iOS and Android needs to be completely different. For example, *Material Design* introduced the concept of a *Floating Action Button* (FAB), like the pink plus-sign button shown in Figure 5-1.

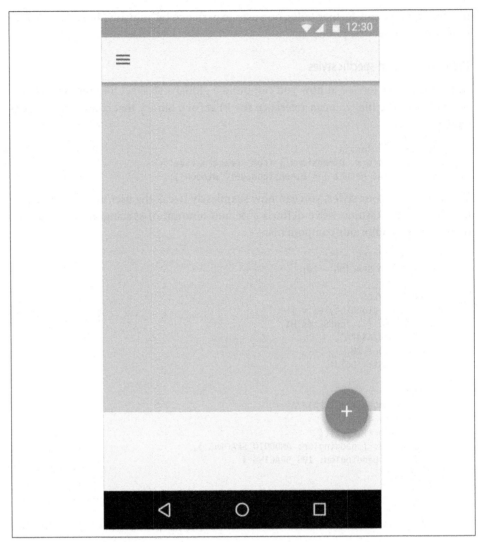

Figure 5-1. The Floating Action Button

This interaction is completely different than in the Apple User Experience Guidelines (*https://apple.co/2FUs80M*).

We can implement the same functionality with a completely different component design by using folders and platform suffixes:

```
components
├─ actionButton
    ├─ index.android.js
    └─ index.ios.js
```

The <ActionButton /> is called in the main *App.js* file:

```
import React, { Component } from 'react';
import {
  StyleSheet,
  View,
  ScrollView,
  Text
} from 'react-native';

import ActionButton from './components/actionButton';

export default class App extends Component<{}> {

  constructor(props) {
    super(props);
    this.state = { times: 0 }
  }

  render() {
    return <View style={styles.container}>
      <View style={styles.header}></View>
      <ScrollView style={styles.scroll}>
        <Text style={styles.text} >Called: {this.state.times} Time(s)</Text>
      </ScrollView>
      <ActionButton onPress={ () => {
      this.setState((prevState) => {
      return { times: prevState.times + 1 };
      });
      } } />
    </View>
  }
}

const styles = StyleSheet.create({
  container: {
    flex: 10,
  },
  text: {
    fontSize: 34
  }
  header: {
    backgroundColor: '#CACACA',
    height: 75
  },
  scroll: {
    height: 200,
  }
});
```

Each platform renders the <ActionButton /> differently:

```
// components/actionButton/index.ios.js
import React, { Component } from 'react';
import {
  StyleSheet,
  TouchableNativeFeedback,
  View,
  Text
} from 'react-native';

export default function ({ onPress }) {
  return <TouchableNativeFeedback onPress={onPress}>
    <View style={styles.button}>
      <Text style={styles.text}> Action! </Text>
    </View>
  </TouchableNativeFeedback>
}

const styles = StyleSheet.create({
  button: {
    borderColor: '#2A547A',
    borderWidth: 1,
    borderRadius: 5,
  },
  text: {
    textAlign: 'center',
    padding: 10,
    color: '#2A547A',
  }
});
```

The Android version of the <ActionBar /> uses Android-specific styles, like eleva
tion, to create the raised button effect:

```
// components/actionButton/index.android.js
import React, { Component } from 'react';
import {
  StyleSheet,
  TouchableHighlight,
  Text
} from 'react-native';

export default function ({ onPress }) {
  return <TouchableHighlight style={styles.button} onPress={onPress}>
    <Text style={styles.text}>+</Text>
  </TouchableHighlight>
}

const styles = StyleSheet.create({
  button: {
    position: 'absolute',
    bottom: 50,
    right: 50,
    backgroundColor: '#ED5281',
```

```
      width: 60,
      height: 60,
      justifyContent: 'center',
      borderRadius: 30,
      elevation: 10,
    },
    text: {
      textAlign: 'center',
      color: '#FFF',
      fontSize: 30,
    }

});
```

Each platform will render based on a look that is more in line with the platform user experience guidelines (Figure 5-2).

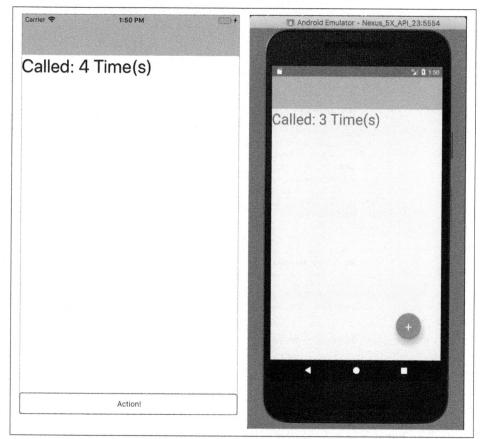

Figure 5-2. Try to follow the user interface guidelines for each platform—here, the same action button is rendered entirely differently on iOS and Android

You are logging Redux events in development only

In Recipe 4.3, we used the `redux-logger` to display state changes in our application to the React Native developer console. The `redux-logger` will start logging all these events in your web browser's developer console like in Figure 5-3.

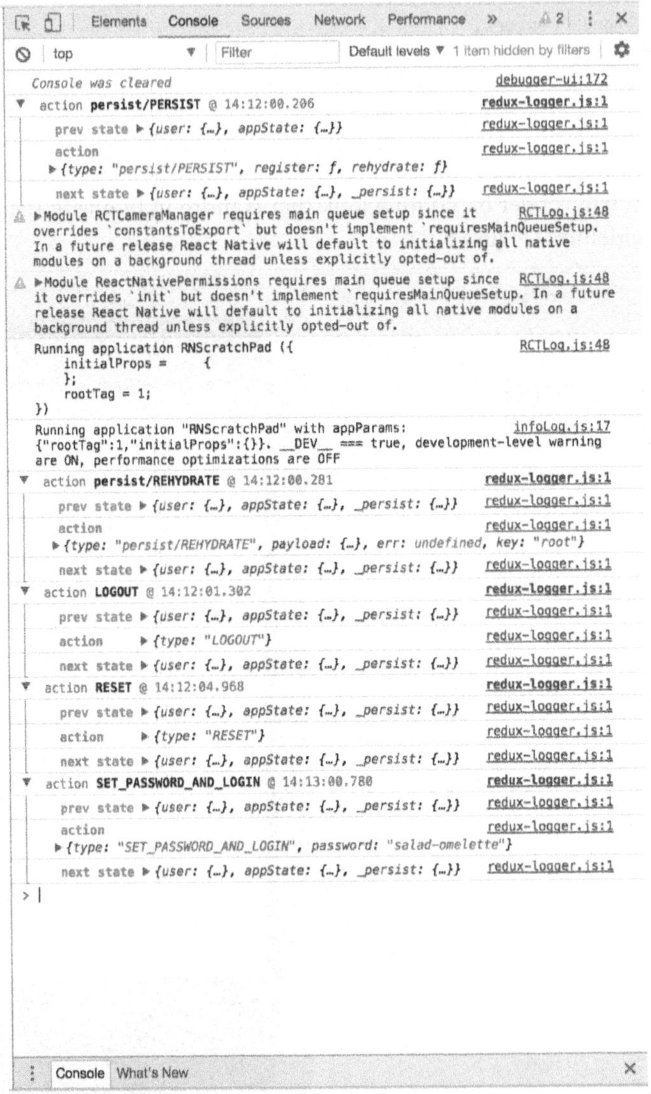

Figure 5-3. Output from redux-logger in the React Native debugger

Accessing these state changes on a device in production would be far beyond the scope of redux-logger. The __DEV__ will return true in development and false in any other case. Let's turn it off in production. Update *reduxStore.js* like so:

```
import * as reducers from './src/reducers';
import { createStore, applyMiddleware, combineReducers, compose} from 'redux';
import { persistCombineReducers } from 'redux-persist';
import storage from 'redux-persist/es/storage';
import logger from 'redux-logger';
const config = {
  key: 'root',
  storage,
};
export default createStore(
  persistCombineReducers(config, reducers),
  __DEV__ ? {} : applyMiddleware(logger)
);
```

Determine whether the app is running on a tablet or a phone

In some cases you will want to render different application components based on whether the device is a tablet or a phone. Begin by installing react-native-device-info:

```
$> npm i --save react-native-device-info
$> react-native link
```

Here is an example of how you might use DeviceInfo.isTablet() to render the correct sidebar component:

```
import React, { Component } from 'react';
import {
  Text,
  View,
  Platform
} from 'react-native';

import DeviceInfo from 'react-native-device-info';

export default class App extends Component {
  narrowSidebar() {
    return <View style={{width: 40, backgroundColor: '#333',
    flexDirection: 'column' }}>
        <View style={{height: 40, backgroundColor: '#666',
        flexDirection: 'row' }}></View>
        <View style={{flex: 0.7 }}></View>
      <View style={{flex: 0.1, backgroundColor: '#000' }}></View>
    </View>
  }
```

```
widesidebar() {
  return <View style={{ flex: 0.2, backgroundColor: '#333' }}>
    <View style={{ flex: 0.2, backgroundColor: '#666',
    flexDirection: 'row' }}>
      <View style={{ width: 50, padding: 5, backgroundColor: '#000' }}>
        <View style={{ width: 40, height: 40, borderRadius: 40,
          justifyContent: "center",
          backgroundColor: "#EA0" }}>
        </View>
      </View>
    </View>
    <View style={{ flex: 0.8 }}></View>
  </View>
}

render() {
  return (
    <View style={{ flexDirection: 'row', flex: 1, backgroundColor: '#FFF' }}>
      {DeviceInfo.isTablet() ? this.wideSidebar() : this.narrowSidebar()  }
      <View style={{ flex: 0.5, backgroundColor: '#FFF' }}>
        <Text>{DeviceInfo.isTablet() ? "Tablet" : "Phone"}</Text>
      </View>
      <View style={{ flex: 0.1, backgroundColor: '#FFA' }}></View>
    </View>
  );
}
}
```

See Also

Another change you may wish to monitor is the device orientation. Fortunately every
`<View />` component includes an `onLayout` property. Learn more in a blog post by
Matthew Sessions (*http://bit.ly/2nICcDy*).

CHAPTER 6

Making Your App Maintainable

As soon as there is more than one software developer working on a project, maintaining consistency across your code base will become a serious consideration. The majority of the examples in this cookbook were stripped to the essentials: no PropTypes, no test cases, no type hints. The strategies for ensuring your code is well factored, easily maintained, and correct are varied, and I hope the approaches discussed here save you from dreadful runtime errors, system bugs, and hermetic coding styles.

6.1 Protect Your Components with PropTypes

Many software developers find that their components written for one purpose are being reused elsewhere for different purposes. For example, you might have designed an information card or a special button for a login form and are now repurposing the same component in an account profile screen.

When a component goes from being used in one context to a completely different one, strange things can happen. Bugs can start appearing from unexpected variations in the properties passed down to these components.

Problem

You are trying to establish a contract for your component. For everything to function correctly, your component must throw an error unless it receives the correct *props* from its parent. Other solutions exist, such as TypeScript or Reason. But *design by contract* or *defensive programming* is a well-established programming pattern for reducing bugs. In a language like JavaScript, we need all the help we can get.

Solution

We are going to refactor the *Pastry Picker* component first developed in Recipe 2.3 into a few smaller components so that we can explore how prop-types can protect us from programmer error.

Begin by adding the prop-types package to your project:

```
$>npm -i prop-types --save
```

 PropTypes are a React convention and have more to do with React than React Native. However, they still are useful in raising errors during development instead of in front of our users.

I have refactored the <PastryPicker /> component to rely on two smaller components, a <PastryButton /> that enables switching recipes and an <IngredientBar /> for rendering the actual bar chart:

```
// pastryPicker.js
import React, { Component } from 'react';
import {
  StyleSheet,
  View,
} from 'react-native';

import IngredientBar from './ingredientBar'
import PastryButton from './pastryButton'

const PASTRIES = {
  croissant:    { label: "Croissants",  flour: 0.7, butter: 0.5,
  sugar: 0.2, eggs: 0 },
  cookie:       { label: "Cookies",     flour: 0.5, butter: 0.4,
  sugar: 0.5, eggs: 0.2},
  pancake:      { label: "Pancakes",    flour: 0.7, butter: 0.5,
  sugar: 0.3, eggs: 0.3 },
  doughnut:     { label: "Dougnuts",    flour: 0.5, butter: 0.2,
  sugar: 0.8, eggs: 0.1 },
}

export default class PastryPicker extends Component {
  constructor(props) {
    super(props);
    this.state = {
      selectedPastry: 'croissant'
    }
  }

  setPastry = (selectedPastry) => {
    this.setState({ selectedPastry });
```

```
    }

  render() {
    const { flour, butter, sugar, eggs } = PASTRIES[this.state.selectedPastry];
    return <View style={styles.pastryPicker}>
        <View style={styles.buttons}>
          {
            Object.keys(PASTRIES).map( (key) => <PastryButton key={key}
                isActive={this.state.selectedPastry === key}
                onPress={() => { this.setPastry(key) } }
                label={PASTRIES[key].label} /> )
          }
        </View>
      <View style={styles.ingredientContainer}>
        <IngredientBar backgroundColor="#F2D8A6" flex={flour} label="Flour" />
        <IngredientBar backgroundColor="#FFC049" flex={butter} label="Butter" />
        <IngredientBar backgroundColor="#CACACA" flex={sugar} label="Sugar" />
        <IngredientBar backgroundColor="#FFDE59" flex={eggs} label="Eggs" />
      </View>
    </View>
  }
}


const styles = StyleSheet.create({
  pastryPicker: {
    flex: 1,
    flexDirection: 'column',
    margin: 20,
  },
  ingredientContainer: {
    flex: 1,
    flexDirection: 'row',
  },
  ingredientColumn: {
    flexDirection: 'column',
    flex: 1,
    justifyContent: 'flex-end',
  },
  buttons: {
    flexDirection: 'column',
    flexWrap: "wrap",
    paddingRight: 20,
    paddingLeft: 20,
    flex: 0.3,
  },
});
```

The <PastryButton /> now declares propTypes before export:

```
import React, { Component } from 'react';
import {
  StyleSheet,
```

```
  Text,
  TouchableHighlight,
  View,
} from 'react-native';

import PropTypes from 'prop-types'

class PastryButton extends Component {

  render() {
    const { isActive, onPress, label} = this.props
    return <View style={styles.buttonContainer}>
      <TouchableHighlight onPress={onPress} style={[styles.button, {
        backgroundColor: isActive ? "#CD7734" : "#54250B" } ]}
        underlayColor={"#CD7734"}>
        <Text style={styles.buttonText} >{label}</Text>
      </TouchableHighlight>
    </View>
  }

}

PastryButton.propTypes = {
  isActive: PropTypes.bool,
  label: PropTypes.string.isRequired,
  onPress: PropTypes.func.isRequired,
}

PastryButton.defaultProps = {
  isActive: false
};

export default PastryButton;

const styles = StyleSheet.create({
  button: {
    padding: 10,
    minWidth: 140,
    justifyContent: 'center',
    backgroundColor: "#5A8282",
    borderRadius: 10,
  },
  buttonContainer: {
    margin: 10,
  },
  buttonText: {
    fontSize: 18,
    color: "#FFF",
  },
});
```

Notice how `propTypes` can be either optional or required. A default value can also be supplied as part of `defaultProps`:

```
// ingredientBar.js
import React, { Component } from 'react';
import {
  Animated,
  StyleSheet,
  Text,
  TouchableHighlight,
  View,
} from 'react-native';

import PropTypes from 'prop-types';

class IngredientBar extends Component {

  render() {
    const { backgroundColor, flex, label } = this.props;
    return <View style={styles.ingredientColumn}>
      <View style={styles.bar} />
      <View style={{ backgroundColor, flex }} />
      <View style={styles.label}><Text>{label}</Text></View>
    </View>
  }

}

IngredientBar.propTypes = {
  backgroundColor: PropTypes.string.isRequired,
  label: PropTypes.string.isRequired,
  flex: PropTypes.number.isRequired,
}

export default IngredientBar;

const styles = StyleSheet.create({
  ingredientColumn: {
    flexDirection: 'column',
    flex: 1,
    justifyContent: 'flex-end',
  },
  bar: {
    alignSelf: 'flex-start',
    flexGrow: 0,
  },
  label: {
    flex: 0.2,
  },
});
```

With a few extra lines of code, we can sleep well knowing that our `<PastryButton />` and `<IngredientBar />` will raise warnings unless they receive the props they expect.

Discussion

When React was first unveiled, *PropTypes* were part of the package: a simple, declarative way of enforcing which arguments needed to be given to a React component. As React evolved in the public, the `prop-types` package became a separate NPM package and other solutions to the same problem emerged.

See Also

PropTypes can get far more sophisticated when dealing with a deeply nested data structure (like from a GraphQL API). The React.js guide for PropTypes (*http://bit.ly/2nQuRkt*) covers many of the examples you may face when implementing your own PropTypes.

6.2 Check Runtime Errors with Flow

The PropTypes package provides a great safety harness for building and delivering React components, but we can do so much better.

Writing a `propTypes` declaration forces you to think about the boundary of your component: how will it be used? What are acceptable inputs and when should I raise a warning? Unfortunately some of these cases are hard to identify given the dynamic nature of JavaScript's runtime environment.

Problem

Can we catch more bugs during the compilation step and avoid more unhappy users? Writing PropTypes is a bit of extra work, but we can already see how it might pay off. If we are already invested in trying to improve the type checking and contract between our components and the broader application, are there better tools at our disposal? How can we ensure that every single function, class, and variable is *type safe*?

Flow (*https://flow.org*) provides a simple-to-use development tool. It takes minutes to set up and will improve your overall development experience in no time.

Solution

Before we install Flow, we should understand the specific challenge it tackles: ensuring that input is of the correct type. Flow does this by tracing through your code paths and veryfing that every class, function, and variable assignment is the correct type. Flow is not focused on coding standards or style. You will also notice that by default, Flow will only look at files that begin with // @*flow*.

When Flow is correctly installed, the following code will trigger an error:

```
// @flow
// test.js
const butterQuantity = "6 cups"
const doubleButter = butterQuantity * 2
```

The Flow server returns with:

```
Error: test.js:4
  4: const doubleButter = butterQuantity * 2
                          ^^^^^^^^^^^^^^ string. The operand of an arithmetic
                          operation must be a number.
```

Flow won't stop me from doubling my `butterQuantity`, but it will stop me from multiplying a `string` with a `number`.

Run Flow from the command line by typing `yarn run flow` before committing code and pushing it to your source code repository. This way, team members will be sure that everything is being run as expected. Flow can save you from embarrassing programming mistakes or spending time in code reviews discussing issues that Flow can catch. You can also set up Flow in a development environment like *Nuclide*, *Sublime Text*, or *Visual Studio Code*.

Flow's documentation assumes you are using Yarn for your package management needs. In general I prefer Yarn and have chosen to use it instead of NPM. See Recipe 1.1 for more information about Yarn and NPM.

Setting up Flow

Start by adding Flow and initializing a *.flowconfig* file in your project folder:

```
$> yarn add --dev flow-bin
$> yarn run flow init
```

In order to make a code comparison possible, I decided to refactor the `react-native-pastry-picker` project to use Flow instead of `PropTypes`, like in Recipe 6.1. Flow and `PropTypes` try to protect you from the same family of coding errors. This way you can see how each one addresses the challenge through syntax.

Before adjusting *App.js*, *ingredientBar.js*, and *pastryButton.js*, I had to make some additional project configuration changes. Because `react-native-pastry-picker` is an NPM package that does not have a locked `react-native` dependency, Flow will mistakenly raise an error for `react-native` when running `yarn run flow`:

```
Error: ingredientBar.js:9
  9: } from 'react-native';
              ^^^^^^^^^^^^^^ react-native. Required module not found

Error: pastryButton.js:8
  8: } from 'react-native';
              ^^^^^^^^^^^^^^ react-native. Required module not found

Error: pastryPicker.js:6
  6: } from 'react-native';
              ^^^^^^^^^^^^^^ react-native. Required module not found
```

By adding flow-typed under [libs] in the *.flowconfig* configuration file, and relaxing the react-native dependency, I can remove these errors:

```
# .flowconfig
[ignore]

[include]

[libs]
flow-typed

[lints]

[options]

[strict]
```

Now create a folder called */flow-typed/* and include a new file, */flow-typed/react-native.js*:

```
declare module 'react-native' {
  declare module.exports: any;
}
```

This declaration will configure Flow to check the */flow-typed* folder for any missing modules before throwing an exception.

The *ingredientBar.js* file can now be updated with Flow type hints. Notice that the type Props declaration provides type checking for the entire component. PropTypes are no longer required:

```
// @flow
import React, { Component } from 'react';
import {
  Animated,
  StyleSheet,
  Text,
  TouchableHighlight,
  View,
} from 'react-native';
```

```
type Props = {
  backgroundColor: string,
  label: string,
  flex: number
}

export default class IngredientBar extends Component<Props>{

  render() {
    const { backgroundColor, flex, label } = this.props;
    return <View style={styles.ingredientColumn}>
      <View style={styles.bar} />
      <View style={{ backgroundColor, flex }} />
      <View style={styles.label}><Text>{label}</Text></View>
    </View>
  }

}

const styles = StyleSheet.create({
  ingredientColumn: {
    flexDirection: 'column',
    flex: 1,
    justifyContent: 'flex-end',
  },
  bar: {
    alignSelf: 'flex-start',
    flexGrow: 0,
  },
  label: {
    flex: 0.2,
  },
});
```

The `<PastryButton />` component supports an optional `isActive` type, which Flow represents with `isActive?: bool`. The `?` indicates that this is a default attribute. Functions also have a specific signature, which includes the number of arguments, their expected type, and whether they should return a value. For example, `onPress: (key: string) => void` indicates that the `onPress` callback will accept one argument (a string) and not return anything (void):

```
// @flow
import React, { Component } from 'react';
import {
  StyleSheet,
  Text,
  TouchableHighlight,
  View,
} from 'react-native';

type Props = {
```

```
    isActive?: bool,
    label: string,
    onPress: (key: string) => void
}

export default class PastryButton extends Component<Props>{

    static defaultProps = {
      isActive: false
    }

    render() {
      const { isActive, onPress, label} = this.props
      return <View style={styles.buttonContainer}>
        <TouchableHighlight onPress={onPress} style={[styles.button, {
          backgroundColor: isActive ? "#CD7734" : "#54250B" } ]}
          underlayColor={"#CD7734"}>
          <Text style={styles.buttonText} >{label}</Text>
        </TouchableHighlight>
      </View>
    }

}

const styles = StyleSheet.create({
    button: {
      padding: 10,
      minWidth: 140,
      justifyContent: 'center',
      backgroundColor: "#5A8282",
      borderRadius: 10,
    },
    buttonContainer: {
      margin: 10,
    },
    buttonText: {
      fontSize: 18,
      color: "#FFF",
    },
});
```

While <PastryPicker /> does not have any incoming Props, it does maintain the local state for which pastry is selected. Flow provides similar type checking for State. The PastryPicker component accepts State as a second argument in the declaration Component<{}, State>. This State key indicates that the component will be maintaining a this.state variable. Flow can now protect us from inadvertently manipulating other local state variables that were not defined in the type State:

```
// @flow
import React, { Component } from 'react';
import {
```

```
  StyleSheet,
  View,
} from 'react-native';

import IngredientBar from './ingredientBar'
import PastryButton from './pastryButton'

const PASTRIES = {
  croissant:    { label: 'Croissants',   flour: 0.7, butter: 0.5,
  sugar: 0.2, eggs: 0 },
  cookie:       { label: 'Cookies',      flour: 0.5, butter: 0.4,
  sugar: 0.5, eggs: 0.2},
  pancake:      { label: 'Pancakes',     flour: 0.7, butter: 0.5,
  sugar: 0.3, eggs: 0.3 },
  doughnut:     { label: 'Dougnuts',     flour: 0.5, butter: 0.2,
  sugar: 0.8, eggs: 0.1 },
}

type State = {
  selectedPastry: string
}

export default class PastryPicker extends Component<{}, State> {
  state: State

  constructor(props: {}) {
    super(props);
    this.state = {
      selectedPastry: 'croissant'
    }
  }

  setPastry = (selectedPastry: string) => {
    this.setState({ selectedPastry });
  }

  render() {
    const { flour, butter, sugar, eggs } = PASTRIES[this.state.selectedPastry];
    return <View style={styles.pastryPicker}>
        <View style={styles.buttons}>
          {
            Object.keys(PASTRIES).map( (key) => <PastryButton key={key}
                isActive={this.state.selectedPastry === key}
                onPress={() => { this.setPastry(key) } }
                label={PASTRIES[key].label} /> )
          }
        </View>
      <View style={styles.ingredientContainer}>
        <IngredientBar backgroundColor='#F2D8A6' flex={flour} label='Flour' />
        <IngredientBar backgroundColor='#FFC049' flex={butter}
        label='Butter' />
        <IngredientBar backgroundColor='#CACACA' flex={sugar} label='Sugar' />
```

```
            <IngredientBar backgroundColor='#FFDE59' flex={eggs} label='Eggs' />
        </View>
      </View>
    }
  }

  const styles = StyleSheet.create({
    pastryPicker: {
      flex: 1,
      flexDirection: 'column',
      margin: 20,
    },
    ingredientContainer: {
      flex: 1,
      flexDirection: 'row',
    },
    ingredientColumn: {
      flexDirection: 'column',
      flex: 1,
      justifyContent: 'flex-end',
    },
    buttons: {
      flexDirection: 'column',
      flexWrap: 'wrap',
      paddingRight: 20,
      paddingLeft: 20,
      flex: 0.3,
    },
  });
```

Try changing `this.setPastry(key)` to return anything except a string and Flow will raise an error.

See Also

Flow grew out of the React ecosystem as a powerful approach to type safety. Take a look at the Flow Getting Started guide (*https://flow.org/en/docs/getting-started/*) to learn more about what it can do for your unique project requirements. Some folks prefer using *TypeScript*, a language that provides a superset of features on top of ES6+, like interfaces, generics, enums, etc. With all these additional code hints, development environments like Visual Studio Code are able to provide autocomplete and deeper type-checking features. If you are starting a large project, read the TypeScript 5 minute guide (*http://bit.ly/2ENPeqQ*) and determine if it's right for your team.

6.3 Automate Your Component Tests

Unit tests are one of the first things I look for in an open source library. Did the developers take the time to define how the individual code modules were supposed to

---

function? Unit tests provide clues into how a package is designed and intended to be used downstream. Unit tests are very simple functions that pick apart your project and ensure that the input into a function or class results in the desired output. They can never exhaust every possible case, but they improve quality in the following ways:

1. Developers have to write a second *consumer* of their code: the unit test.
2. Code tends to be better factored and the *Single Responsibility Principle* emerges automatically.
3. Unit tests provide a kind of documented intent for how the code should behave. When the documentation fails you, look at the unit tests.

Code quality and maintainability are improved when you combine Flow, ESLint, and a battery of unit tests with *Jest*. Each tool protects you from a specific kind of development challenge.

Problem

How do we set up component tests in React Native? Unit testing ES6+ in general can be done with a number of libraries (like Mocha (*http://bit.ly/2nIxcyF*)), but Jest (*http://bit.ly/2C18TR7*) is the preferred testing framework for React.js. Let's start writing some component tests with Jest for the react-native-pastry-picker project.

Solution

This configuration enables Flow to coexist with Jest. In the following section, we will finish off the example with ESLint for code linting. By combining these technologies, we will have a comprehensive suite of code-quality tooling. Until now, the react-native-pastry-picker library did not have an explicit dependency on react or react-native. Because Jest will be running this code in a test harness, we now require these additional development dependencies.

I will perform two kinds of unit tests. *Snapshot tests*, where Jest generates a data structure representation of the React component in a given state. The *Enzyme test* extension will allow us to inspect the internal state of our subcomponents.

Begin by installing React and React Native (in the case of a package), then Jest and finally Enzyme and the Enzyme adapter:

```
$> npm install --save-dev react react-native
$> npm install --save-dev jest
$> npm install --save-dev enzyme enzyme-adapter-react-16 react-dom
```

As you can imagine, there is a lot of churn around React, React Native, Enzyme, Jest, and Flow. This mix of open source projects has had breaking changes in the past and may in the future. At the time of this writing, the following snippets show a successful set of configuration options. If you find yourself getting stuck, try looking at the GitHub issues for the relevant projects.

The *package.json*:

```json
{
  "name": "react-native-pastry-picker",
  "version": "1.0.5",
  "description": "Pastry Picker",
  "repository": "https://github.com/jlebensold/react-native-pastry-picker",
  "main": "index.js",
  "scripts": {
    "test": "jest"
  },
  "keywords": [
    "react-native"
  ],
  "author": "Jon Lebensold",
  "license": "MIT",
  "devDependencies": {
    "enzyme": "^3.2.0",
    "enzyme-adapter-react-16": "^1.1.0",
    "flow-bin": "^0.59.0",
    "jest": "^21.2.1",
    "jest-cli": "^21.2.1",
    "react": "^16.0.0",
    "react-dom": "^16.1.1",
    "react-native": "^0.50.3",
    "react-test-renderer": "^16.1.1"
  },
  "dependencies": {},
  "jest": {
    "preset": "react-native"
  }
}
```

The *.flowconfig*:

```
[ignore]

; We fork some components by platform
.*/*[.]android.js

; Ignore templates for 'react-native init'
.*/local-cli/templates/.*

; Ignore the website subdir
<PROJECT_ROOT>/website/.*
```

```
; Ignore the Dangerfile
<PROJECT_ROOT>/danger/dangerfile.js

; Ignore "BUCK" generated dirs
<PROJECT_ROOT>/\.buckd/

; Ignore unexpected extra "@providesModule"
.*/node_modules/.*/node_modules/fbjs/.*

; Ignore duplicate module providers
; For RN Apps installed via npm, "Libraries" folder is inside
; "node_modules/react-native" but in the source repo it is in the root
.*/Libraries/react-native/React.js

; Ignore polyfills
.*/Libraries/polyfills/.*

.*/node_modules/react-native/Libraries/react-native/
  react-native-implementation.js

[include]

[libs]
node_modules/react-native/Libraries/react-native/react-native-interface.js
flow-typed/

[options]
emoji=true
module.system=haste
munge_underscores=true
suppress_type=$FlowIssue
suppress_type=$FlowFixMe
suppress_type=$FixMe
unsafe.enable_getters_and_setters=true

[version]
^0.59.0
```

In order for Jest to succesfully parse JSX, I also include a *.babelrc* configuration file in the project root:

```
{
  "presets": ["react-native"]
}
```

In Recipe 6.2, we created a special */flow-typed/react-native.js* file for Flow to use in its dependency checking. Jest will need a similar file in order to avoid any irrelevant errors:

```
// flow-typed/jest.js
declare module 'jest' {
  declare module.exports: any;
```

```
}
declare var expect: any;
declare var test: any;
```

Flow should continue to run as expected with yarn run flow. Now let's create our first Snapshot test. The convention is to include tests in a *__tests__/* folder.

Start with a snapshot of the <PastryPicker /> component:

```
// __tests__/pastryPicker.test.js
// @flow
import React from 'react';
import renderer from 'react-test-renderer';

import PastryPicker from '../pastryPicker';

test('renders correctly', () => {
  const tree = renderer.create(
    <PastryPicker />
  ).toJSON();
  expect(tree).toMatchSnapshot();
});
```

Now run yarn run jest:

```
yarn run jest __tests__/pastryPicker.test.js
yarn run v1.1.0
$ "./react-native-pastry-picker/node_modules/.bin/jest"
"__tests__/pastryPicker.test.js"
 PASS  __tests__/pastryPicker.test.js
  ✓ renders correctly (136ms)

 › 1 snapshot written.
Snapshot Summary
 › 1 snapshot written in 1 test suite.

Test Suites: 1 passed, 1 total
Tests:       1 passed, 1 total
Snapshots:   1 added, 1 total
Time:        0.471s, estimated 1s
```

Jest will write a snapshot of the resulting React component to *__tests__/__snapshots__/pastryPicker.test.js.snap*. Now any further changes to the component will cause the snapshot comparison and the test will fail. This approach ensures any JSX changes result in the necessary side effects. You can refresh the snapshot by running yarn run test -- -u.

This approach to testing is analagous to integration testing: you are testing the overall structure, but don't have deep instrumentation for your component.

The <PastryButton /> will render a different version of the backgroundColor property depending on whether the button isActive. The render() method for <Pastry Button /> looks like this:

```
render() {
  const { isActive, onPress, label} = this.props;
  return <View style={styles.buttonContainer}>
    <TouchableHighlight onPress={onPress} style={[styles.button, {
      backgroundColor: isActive ? '#CD7734' : '#54250B' } ]}
      underlayColor='#CD7734'>
      <Text style={styles.buttonText} >{label}</Text>
    </TouchableHighlight>
  </View>
}
```

Instead of simply comparing the snapshot in its totality, let's see if we can inspect this one state change with the help of Enzyme:

```
// @flow
import React from 'react';
import PastryButton from '../pastryButton';
import renderer from 'react-test-renderer';
import Enzyme, { shallow } from 'enzyme';
import Adapter from 'enzyme-adapter-react-16';
Enzyme.configure({adapter: new Adapter()});

test('renders isActive', () => {
  const tree = renderer.create(
    <PastryButton onPress={ (t) => {} } label='Croissant' isActive={true} />
  ).toJSON();
  expect(tree).toMatchSnapshot();
});

test('when isActive = false, then background = #5A8282', () => {
  const button = shallow(
    <PastryButton onPress={ (t) => {} } label='MyLabel' isActive={false} />);
  expect(button.find('TouchableHighlight').props().style[0].backgroundColor)
    .toEqual('#5A8282');
});
```

The button.find('TouchableHighlight').props().style[0].backgroundColor DOM traversal is similar to browser-based testing with CSS selectors: it can work for testing critical code paths, but it can also be brittle if this is your only means of testing business logic.

Both of these approaches should convince you that it's best to keep as little business logic or application code in your React components as possible. Let your React component focus on rendering and not much more. In this way, the rest of your application can be tested as though it was just plain old ES6+.

Discussion

The *test-driven development* programming movement made every career software developer aware of the importance of writing tests. The saying goes that bugs crop up in untested code. Martin Fowler provides some excellent advice about how much to test (*https://martinfowler.com/bliki/TestCoverage.html*):

> I would say you are doing enough testing if the following is true:
>
> 1. You rarely get bugs that escape into production, and
>
> 2. You are rarely hesitant to change some code for fear it will cause production bugs.
>
> Can you test too much? Sure you can. You are testing too much if you can remove tests while still having enough. But this is a difficult thing to sense. One sign you are testing too much is if your tests are slowing you down.
>
> —Martin Fowler, *Test Coverage*
> (17 April 2012)

See Also

Testing is a broad subject and this primer only scratches the surface. From here, you may find it helpful to *mock* some of the native components or any other asynchronous actions that your application may take. The Jest React Native Tutorial (*http://bit.ly/2sdVllD*) covers a handful of use cases worth considering.

You may also want to dig into Jest's code coverage reports. Of course, all of these commands could also be run using a *continuous integration* service like Jenkins, CircleCI, or Codeship every time a developer pushes code to your source code repository. You are on your way to deploying new versions of your app with greater and greater confidence that old bugs won't reappear in new builds.

6.4 Maintain Coding Standards with ESLint

Consistent code is criticial to ensuring that a software developer can feel at home in any part of the code base. Honey and maple syrup are both capable of sweetening a dish, but mixing them together will probably lead to loss of the unique flavors achieved with either sweetener. The same is true with code: mixing tabs and spaces, *camelCase*, and *snake_case* in the same code base leaves the software developer's palette wanting.

Problem

How do you make sure that your project feels like it was written by one author? A good ESLint rule set will protect every member of the team from each other and yourself.

Solution

Begin by adding ESLint to your project. Airbnb has published an excellent JavaScript style guide (*http://bit.ly/2EKaEF3*). It has gone above and beyond and provided a set of linting tools that can easily be incorporated into any React Native project.

Start by installing ESLint:

```
$> npm install --save-dev eslint
$> ./node_modules/.bin/eslint --init
```

You will then be prompted to select how to configure ESLint. For my project, I chose:

- How would you like to configure ESLint? *Use a popular style guide*
- Which style guide do you want to follow? *Airbnb*
- Do you use React? (y/N) *y*
- What format do you want your config file to be in? *JSON*

 ESlint works best when you can give it a handful of folders to run against. I recommend putting your React Native project code in a folder like *src/*. You can then simplify your ESLint script. For the react-native-pastry-picker project, I have moved all the components into *src/*.

Because my project includes a collection of flow types from Recipe 6.2, some additional configuration is required. Fortunately, the `eslint-plugin-flowtype` package (*http://bit.ly/2EsowWI*) makes the integration between ESLint and Flow seamless:

```
npm install babel-eslint --save-dev
npm install eslint-plugin-flowtype --save-dev
```

`babel-eslint` is a special ESLint parser that will properly account for the Flow type hints in your project. `eslint-plugin-flowtype` includes a collection of additional ESLint rules. Layer on additional ESLint rules that account for Flow's extended type hints by updating the *.eslintrc.json* file:

```
{
  "parser": "babel-eslint",
  "extends": "airbnb",
  "plugins": [
    "flowtype"
  ],
  "rules": {
    "flowtype/boolean-style": [
      2,
      "boolean"
    ],
```

```
    "flowtype/define-flow-type": 1,
    "flowtype/delimiter-dangle": [
      2,
      "never"
    ],
    "flowtype/generic-spacing": [
      2,
      "never"
    ],
    "flowtype/no-primitive-constructor-types": 2,
    "flowtype/no-types-missing-file-annotation": 2,
    "flowtype/no-weak-types": 2,
    "flowtype/object-type-delimiter": [
      2,
      "comma"
    ],
    "flowtype/require-parameter-type": 2,
    "flowtype/require-return-type": [
      2,
      "always",
      {
        "annotateUndefined": "never"
      }
    ],
    "flowtype/require-valid-file-annotation": 2,
    "flowtype/semi": [
      2,
      "always"
    ],
    "flowtype/space-after-type-colon": [
      2,
      "always"
    ],
    "flowtype/space-before-generic-bracket": [
      2,
      "never"
    ],
    "flowtype/space-before-type-colon": [
      2,
      "never"
    ],
    "flowtype/type-id-match": [
      2,
      "^([A-Z][a-z0-9]+)+Type$"
    ],
    "flowtype/union-intersection-spacing": [
      2,
      "always"
    ],
    "flowtype/use-flow-type": 1,
    "flowtype/valid-syntax": 1
  },
```

```
      "settings": {
        "flowtype": {
          "onlyFilesWithFlowAnnotation": false
        }
      }
    }
```

By running *node_modules/eslint/bin/eslint.js*, you should start to see all the inconsistencies in your source code:

```
/Users/jon/Projects/react-native-pastry-picker/src/ingredientBar.js
   4:3    err. 'Animated' is defined but ...      no-unused-vars
   7:3    err. 'TouchableHighlight' is de...      no-unused-vars
  12:1    err. Type identifier 'Props' do...      flowtype/type-id-match
  18:16   err. Component should be written...     react/prefer-stateless-function
  19:9    err. Missing return type annotation     flowtype/require-return-type
  21:13   err. JSX not allowed in files with...   react/jsx-filename-extension
  21:26   err. 'styles' was used before it was... no-use-before-define
  22:20   err. 'styles' was used before it was... no-use-before-define
  24:20   err. 'styles' was used before it was... no-use-before-define
  25:13   err. Expected indentation of 4 space...  react/jsx-indent

/Users/jon/Projects/react-native-pastry-picker/src/pastryButton.js
  10:1    err. Type identifier 'Props' does...    flowtype/type-id-match
  21:9    err. Missing return type annotation     flowtype/require-return-type
  23:13   err. JSX not allowed in files with...   react/jsx-filename-extension
  23:26   err. 'styles' was used before it was... no-use-before-define
  26:17   err. 'styles' was used before it was... no-use-before-define
  29:22   err. 'styles' was used before it was... no-use-before-define
  31:13   err. Expected indentation of 4 space...  react/jsx-indent

/Users/jon/Projects/react-native-pastry-picker/src/pastryPicker.js
  26:1    err. Type identifier 'State' does...    flowtype/type-id-match
  31:3    err. state should be placed after...    react/sort-comp
  44:9    err. Missing return type annotation     flowtype/require-return-type
  48:13   err. JSX not allowed in files with...   react/jsx-filename-extension
  48:26   err. 'styles' was used before it was... no-use-before-define
  49:20   err. 'styles' was used before it was... no-use-before-define
  51:39   err. Missing "key" parameter type...    flowtype/require-parameter-type
  51:39   err. Missing return type annotation     flowtype/require-return-type
  59:20   err. 'styles' was used before it was... no-use-before-define
  65:13   err. Expected indentation of 4 space...  react/jsx-indent

✖ 27 problems (27 errors, 0 warnings)
  3 errors, 0 warnings potentially fixable with the `--fix` option.
```

In just three components, ESLint was able to detect 27 errors! Some of these are style choices that I don't agree with—for example, I don't have a problem including JSX in a file ending in *.js*. Let's disable that rule in our *.eslintrc.json* file:

```
...
"env": {
  "jest": true
```

```
  },
  "rules": {
    "react/jsx-filename-extension": [
      0
    ],
    "import/no-extraneous-dependencies": [
      "error", { "devDependencies": true  }
    ],
    ...
```

By setting react/jsx-filename-extension to [0], ESLint will now ignore this rule. I also want to run eslint on my test suite, which relies on a few global functions. To ignore them, add "jest": true as part of your environment. Because the react-native-pastry-picker is an external package, certain dependencies, like react and react-native, are devDependencies. Relaxing the import/no-extraneous-dependencies rule is required because it will be imported into other React Native applications with their own dependencies on react and react-native.

By rerunning the linter, my error set has dropped to 24 errors.

The following three components, after ESLint and Flow checking, now all follow a consistent style. Note that the implementation has not changed at all—ESLint detected that the <IngredientBar /> component could be refactored into a pure function:

```
// src/ingredientBar.js
// @flow
import React, { type Element } from 'react';
import {
  StyleSheet,
  Text,
  View,
} from 'react-native';


type PropType = {
  backgroundColor: string,
  label: string,
  flex: number
};

const styles = StyleSheet.create({
  ingredientColumn: {
    flexDirection: 'column',
    flex: 1,
    justifyContent: 'flex-end',
  },
  bar: {
    alignSelf: 'flex-start',
    flexGrow: 0,
  },
  label: {
```

```
      flex: 0.2,
    },
  });

  export default function IngredientBar({ backgroundColor, flex, label }:
  PropType):
    Element<View> {
    return (
      <View style={styles.ingredientColumn}>
        <View style={styles.bar} />
        <View style={{ backgroundColor, flex }} />
        <View style={styles.label}><Text>{label}</Text></View>
      </View>
    );
  }
```

The render() method now has a Flow return type:

```
// src/pastryButton.js
// @flow
import React, { Component, type Element } from 'react';
import {
  StyleSheet,
  Text,
  TouchableHighlight,
  View,
} from 'react-native';

type PropType = {
  isActive?: boolean,
  label: string,
  onPress: (key: string) => void
};

const styles = StyleSheet.create({
  button: {
    padding: 10,
    minWidth: 140,
    justifyContent: 'center',
    backgroundColor: '#5A8282',
    borderRadius: 10,
  },
  buttonContainer: {
    margin: 10,
  },
  buttonText: {
    fontSize: 18,
    color: '#FFF',
  },
});

export default class PastryButton extends Component<PropType> {
  static defaultProps = {
```

```
      isActive: false,
    }

  props: PropType

  render(): Element<View> {
    const { isActive, onPress, label } = this.props;
    return (
      <View style={styles.buttonContainer}>
        <TouchableHighlight
          onPress={onPress}
          style={[styles.button, { backgroundColor: isActive ?
          '#CD7734' : '#54250B' }]}
          underlayColor="#CD7734"
        >
          <Text style={styles.buttonText} >{label}</Text>
        </TouchableHighlight>
      </View>);
  }
}
```

ESLint's --fix flag reformatted the PASTRIES constant:

```
// @flow
import React, { Component, type Element } from 'react';
import {
  StyleSheet,
  View,
} from 'react-native';

import IngredientBar from './ingredientBar';
import PastryButton from './pastryButton';

const PASTRIES = {
  croissant: {
    label: 'Croissants', flour: 0.7, butter: 0.5, sugar: 0.2, eggs: 0,
  },
  cookie: {
    label: 'Cookies', flour: 0.5, butter: 0.4, sugar: 0.5, eggs: 0.2,
  },
  pancake: {
    label: 'Pancakes', flour: 0.7, butter: 0.5, sugar: 0.3, eggs: 0.3,
  },
  doughnut: {
    label: 'Dougnuts', flour: 0.5, butter: 0.2, sugar: 0.8, eggs: 0.1,
  },
};

const styles = StyleSheet.create({
  pastryPicker: {
    flex: 1,
    flexDirection: 'column',
    margin: 20,
```

```
    },
    ingredientContainer: {
      flex: 1,
      flexDirection: 'row',
    },
    ingredientColumn: {
      flexDirection: 'column',
      flex: 1,
      justifyContent: 'flex-end',
    },
    buttons: {
      flexDirection: 'column',
      flexWrap: 'wrap',
      paddingRight: 20,
      paddingLeft: 20,
      flex: 0.3,
    },
});

type StateType = {
  selectedPastry: string
};

export default class PastryPicker extends Component<{}, StateType> {
  constructor(props: {}) {
    super(props);
    this.state = {
      selectedPastry: 'croissant',
    };
  }

  state: StateType

  setPastry = (selectedPastry: string) => {
    this.setState({ selectedPastry });
  }

  renderButtons(): Array<View> {
    return Object.keys(PASTRIES).map((key: string): Element<View> =>
    (<PastryButton
      key={key}
      isActive={this.state.selectedPastry === key}
      onPress={() => { this.setPastry(key); }}
      label={PASTRIES[key].label}
    />));
  }

  render(): Element<View> {
    const {
      flour, butter, sugar, eggs,
    } = PASTRIES[this.state.selectedPastry];
```

```
    return (
      <View style={styles.pastryPicker}>
        <View style={styles.buttons}>
          {this.renderButtons()}
        </View>
        <View style={styles.ingredientContainer}>
          <IngredientBar backgroundColor='#F2D8A6' flex={flour} label='Flour' />
          <IngredientBar backgroundColor='#FFC049' flex={butter}
          label='Butter' />
          <IngredientBar backgroundColor='#CACACA' flex={sugar} label='Sugar' />
          <IngredientBar backgroundColor='#FFDE59' flex={eggs} label='Eggs' />
        </View>
      </View>
    );
  }
}
```

You can also try to fix some common errors by running ESLint with the `--fix` flag. Make sure you have committed your source code before it runs so you can verify the changes and make sure that there are no functional differences.

Discussion

With Flow and Jest, you have tools that ensure program correctness, but neither will address style and consistency. ESLint is a powerful tool for ensuring that:

- Variables that have been declared are used
- Spacing rules are respected
- Naming conventions are followed
- Debugging statements like `console.log` or `debugger` are removed
- Semicolons are added (or not)
- Variables are not assigned inside of `if()` statements

Explore all rules ESLint can enforce in its documentation (*http://bit.ly/2GUHhRd*).

See Also

This example only scratches the surface of what ESLint can do to improve the maintainability and code quality of your project. Consider integrating ESLint into your development environment by using the ESLint integrations guide (*http://bit.ly/2nQHsEn*).

6.5 Write Your App with Reason

Reason is a type-safe language built on top of the incredible OCaml compiler. Using BuckleScript (*http://bit.ly/2E4Qqsu*), we can transform OCaml code into JavaScript. There is a small, but incredibly productive community of React Native developers writing apps with Reason.

The Reason website (*https://reasonml.github.io/*) also provides excellent guides and documentation to get you started.

Problem

You have JavaScript fatigue, but you want to build apps with React Native. Tired of dealing with versioning challenges, you want to work with a simpler language that can be compiled and analyzed for its correctness before it becomes JavaScript running on the client. Enter Reason.

Solution

In order to see how the same concepts look with a different implementation, let's rewrite the `react-native-pastry-picker` as a Reason application. The Reason version of the pastry picker has about 15% less code if you factor in the unit tests and flow types.

The PastryPicker component in Figure 6-1 maintains the same functionality, but now benefits from the syntax features in Reason.

Start by adding BuckleScript, ReasonReact, and BuckleScript React Native bindings:

```
$> yarn add bs-platform reason-react bs-react-native
```

Now add a BuckleScript configuration file (*bsconfig.json*) to your project root:

```json
{
  "name": "my-reason",
  "sources": [
    {
      "dir": "src",
      "subdirs": true
    },
  ],
  "refmt": 3,
  "reason": {
    "react-jsx": 2
  },
  "package-specs": [
    {
      "module": "commonjs",
      "in-source": true
    }
```

```
  ],
  "bs-dependencies": [
    "bs-react-native",
    "reason-react",
  ],
  "generate-merlin": true,
  "bsc-flags": ["-bs-super-errors"],
  "suffix": ".bs.js"
}
```

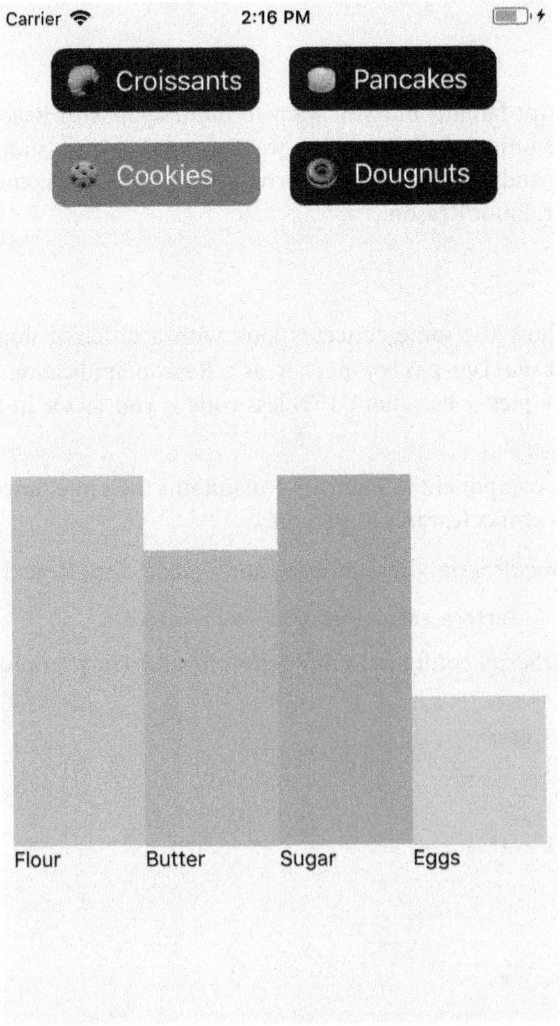

Figure 6-1. The react-native-pastry-picker application

We are also going to need a process that will watch for changes to our Reason files. The watcher will take these *.re* files and convert them into *.bs.js* variants that can be consumed as regular JavaScript by larger React Native applications.

Add `bsb -make-world -w` to the `scripts` in your *package.json*. It might look like this:

```
"scripts": {
  "start": "node node_modules/react-native/local-cli/cli.js start",
  "test": "jest",
  "watch": "bsb -make-world -w"
},
```

The *bsconfig.json* file described tells the BuckleScript compiler to look in the *src/* folder for Reason files.

Let's write a *Hello World* Reason React Native component in *src/hello.re*:

```
open ReactNative;

let component = ReasonReact.statelessComponent("Hello");

let styles =
  StyleSheet.create(
    Style.(
      {
        "text": style([fontSize(18.), color("#00F")])
      }
    )
  );

let make = (~name, _children) => {
  ...component,
    render: (_self) => <Text style=styles##text >(
      ReasonReact.stringToElement({j|Hello, $name |j})
    )</Text>
};

let default = ReasonReact.wrapReasonForJs(
  ~component,
  (jsProps) => make(~name=jsProps##name, [||])
);
```

Start the BuckleScript watcher:

```
$> yarn run watch
```

> If you manage your source code using version control like Git, adding an ignore rule for **.bs.js* files in your *.gitignore* file will avoid unnecessary distribution copies of your Reason components.

You should notice that any compile errors will appear in the watch window as you type out the component. When the component is successfully compiled, an *src/hello.bs.js* file will be generated automatically that will look something like this:

```
// Generated by BUCKLESCRIPT VERSION 2.0.0, PLEASE EDIT WITH CARE
'use strict';

var TextRe       = require("bs-react-native/src/components/textRe.js");
var StyleRe      = require("bs-react-native/src/styleRe.js");
var ReasonReact  = require("reason-react/src/ReasonReact.js");
var StyleSheetRe = require("bs-react-native/src/styleSheetRe.js");

var component = ReasonReact.statelessComponent("Hello");

var styles = StyleSheetRe.create({
    text: StyleRe.style(/* :: */[
        StyleRe.fontSize(18),
        /* :: */[
          StyleRe.color("#00F"),
          /* [] */0
        ]
      ])
  });

function make(name, _) {
  var newrecord = component.slice();
  newrecord[/* render */9] = (function () {
  return ReasonReact.element(/* None */0, /* None */0, TextRe.Text[/* make
  */0](/* None */0, /* None */0, /* None */0, /* None */0, /* None */0,
  /* None
  */0, /* None */0, /* None */0, /* None */0, /* Some */[styles.text],
  /* None
  */0, /* None */0, /* None */0, /* None */0, /* None */0, /* None */0,
  /* None
  */0, /* array */["Hello, " + (String(name) + " ")])));
    });
  return newrecord;
}

var $$default = ReasonReact.wrapReasonForJs(component, (function (jsProps) {
      return make(jsProps.name, /* array */[]);
    }));

exports.component = component;
exports.styles    = styles;
exports.make      = make;
exports.$$default = $$default;
exports.default   = $$default;
exports.__esModule= true;
/* component Not a pure module */
```

Now include the component in your root *App.js* file as if it were any other *.js* file:

```
// App.js
import React, { Component } from 'react';
import {
  StyleSheet,
  View,
} from 'react-native'

import Hello from "./src/hello.bs"

export default class App extends Component<{}> {

  render() {
    return <View style={styles.container}>
      <Hello name="World" />
    </View>
  }
}

const styles = StyleSheet.create({
  container: {
    flex: 1,
    paddingTop: 30,
    backgroundColor: "#FFF",
  }
});
```

In Figure 6-2, you can see a rendering of a "Hello World" application with React Native and Reason.

Figure 6-2. Hello World with Reason and React Native

With all the tooling in place we can now implement <PastryPicker />, <Ingredient Bar />, and <PastryButton />.

The *src/ingredientBar.re* file illustrates simple parameter passing as props. Notice how even the stylesheet is type safe! For example, `flexDirection()` accepts an enum value instead of a string:

```
open ReactNative;

let component = ReasonReact.statelessComponent("IngredientBar");

let styles =
  StyleSheet.create(
    Style.(
      {
        "ingredientColumn":
          style([
            flexDirection(`column),
            flex(1.),
            justifyContent(`flexEnd)
          ]),
        "bar":
          style([
            alignSelf(`flexStart),
            flexGrow(0.)
          ]),
        "label":
          style([
            flex(0.2)
          ])
      }
    )
  );

let make = (~label, ~barColor, ~flexValue, _children) => {
  ...component,
    render: (_self) =>
      Style.(
        <View style=styles##ingredientColumn >
          <View style=styles##bar />
          <View style=(style([backgroundColor(barColor), flex(flexValue) ])) />
          <View style=styles##label>
            <Text>(ReasonReact.stringToElement(label))</Text>
          </View>
        </View>
      )
};

let default = ReasonReact.wrapReasonForJs(
  ~component,
  (jsProps) => make(~label=jsProps##label,
    ~flexValue=jsProps##flexValue, ~barColor=jsProps##barColor, [||]))
```

The *src/pastryButton.re* file illustrates how return values from `if`/`else` conditions can be performed in the context of rendering a stylesheet:

```
open ReactNative;

let component = ReasonReact.statelessComponent("PastryButton");

let styles =
  StyleSheet.create(
    Style.(
      {
        "container":
          style([
            margin(10.),
          ]),
        "button":
          style([
            padding(10.),
            minWidth(140.),
            justifyContent(`center),
            backgroundColor("#5A8282"),
            borderRadius(10.)
          ]),
        "text": style([fontSize(18.), color("#FFF")])
      }
    )
  );

let make = (~label, ~isActive, ~onPress, _children) => {
  ...component,
    render: (_self) =>
      Style.(
        <View style=styles##container >
          <TouchableHighlight onPress
            style=(concat([styles##button, style([
                backgroundColor(
                  if (isActive) {
                    "#CD7734"
                  } else {
                    "#54250B"
                  })
              ])]))
            >
            <Text style=styles##text >(ReasonReact.stringToElement(label))</Text>
          </TouchableHighlight>
        </View>
      )
};

let default = ReasonReact.wrapReasonForJs(
  ~component,
  (jsProps) => make(~label=jsProps##label, ~onPress=jsProps##onPress,
                    ~isActive=jsProps##isActive, [|||])
);
```

The most featureful Reason component in this example is the actual *src/pastry-Picker.re* file. I take full advantage of Reason's type system to build a list of type `pastry`. Like Recipe 2.5, we perform an `action` of `Click(pastry)`. This triggers a reducer on the component to perform a local state change:

```
open ReactNative;

type pastry = {
  label: string,
  flour: float,
  sugar: float,
  butter: float,
  eggs: float,
  isActive: bool
};

type action =
  | Click(pastry);

let pastryList = [
{ label: {j|Croissants|j},  flour: 0.7, butter: 0.5,
               sugar: 0.2, eggs: 0.0, isActive: true },
{ label: {j|Cookies|j},      flour: 0.5, butter: 0.4,
               sugar: 0.5, eggs: 0.2, isActive: false },
{ label: {j|Pancakes|j},  flour: 0.7, butter: 0.5,
               sugar: 0.3, eggs: 0.3, isActive: false },
{ label: {j|Dougnuts|j},  flour: 0.5, butter: 0.2,
               sugar: 0.8, eggs: 0., isActive: false }
];

type state = {
  pastries: list(pastry)
};

let styles =
  StyleSheet.create(
    Style.(
      {
        "pastryPicker":
          style([
            flexDirection(`column),
            flex(1.),
            margin(20.)
          ]),
        "ingredientContainer":
          style([
            flexDirection(`row),
            flex(1.),
          ]),
        "ingredientColumn":
          style([
            flexDirection(`column),
```

```reason
                flex(1.),
                justifyContent(`flexEnd)
              ]),
          "buttons":
            style([
              flexDirection(`column),
              flexWrap(`wrap),
              paddingRight(20.),
              paddingLeft(20.),
              flex(0.3)
            ])
        }
      )
  );

let component = ReasonReact.reducerComponent("pastryPicker");

let make = (_children) => {
  ...component,
  initialState: () => { pastries: pastryList },
  reducer: (action, { pastries }) =>
    switch action {
      | Click(clickedPastry) => ReasonReact.Update({
          pastries:
            pastries
            |> List.map((item) => { ...item,
              isActive: (clickedPastry.label == item.label) })
        });
    },
  render: ({ state, reduce }) => {
    let active = state.pastries
                 |> List.find( (item) => item.isActive);
    <View style=styles##pastryPicker >
      <View style=styles##buttons >
        (
          state.pastries
          |> List.map((item) => <PastryButton isActive=item.isActive
             onPress=(reduce((_event) => Click(item) ))
             key=item.label
             label=item.label />)
          |> Array.of_list
          |> ReasonReact.arrayToElement
        )
      </View>
      <View style=styles##ingredientContainer>
        <IngredientBar barColor="#F2D8A6" flexValue=(active.flour)
        label="Flour" />
        <IngredientBar barColor="#FFC049" flexValue=(active.butter)
        label="Butter" />
        <IngredientBar barColor="#CACACA" flexValue=(active.sugar)
        label="Sugar" />
        <IngredientBar barColor="#FFDE59" flexValue=(active.eggs)
```

```
        label="Eggs" />
      </View>
    </View>
  }
};

let default = ReasonReact.wrapReasonForJs(
  ~component,
  (jsProps) => make([||])
);
```

Now import the PastryPicker with `import PastryPicker from "./src/pastry`
`Picker.bs"` and update your `App.js` `render()` method:

```
render() {
  return <View style={styles.container}>
    <PastryPicker />
  </View>
}
```

Reason would definitely be considered *bleeding edge*, but remember that you are
working with the OCaml compiler, a battle-tested library that has been in development for over two decades. There are some trade-offs to using Reason: the documentation and examples are still changing rapidly and there is a limited set of bindings
and open source packages to draw on. However, Reason is a simpler programming
environment compared to using Flow, Babel, ESLint, etc.

The language itself also has fewer syntactic pecularities when compared to JavaScript.
If you are already using functional languages in your development team or are inter-
ested in building a small, high-performance application team, Reason is worth
considering.

Discussion

Let's face it: JavaScript provides you with a lot of opportunities to make programming
mistakes that will only crop up after your app has been shipped to the various store-
fronts. While Flow, ESLint, TypeScript, and a battery of unit tests will protect you
from a large number of these bugs, why not ditch JavaScript entirely for a language
designed around type safety?

Reason is a statically typed, functional programming language. When you write your
components with Reason, the supercharged OCaml parser will catch programming
errors before you have a chance to switch to your development simulator. Reason's
syntax will be familiar to any modern JavaScript developer. If you have experience
with languages like Lisp, Elixir, Haskell, F#, or Elm, you will feel right at home.

Code is written in Reason, then parsed by the OCaml interpreter and transpiled to
JavaScript with *BuckleScript*, a library that produces performant, safe, and human-
readable JavaScript. With ReasonReact (*http://bit.ly/2C3FS7g*), you can experience the

same productive environment provided by JavaScript. Since this is happening on a native runtime, you still need some special React Native bindings, which are provided by the BuckleScript React Native bindings (*http://bit.ly/2GUJb4f*):

> A type system doesn't magically eliminate bugs; it points out the unhandled conditions and asks you to cover them.
>
> —Reason documentation

Reason's language can also simplify your state management architecture. The unidirectional *Flux* pattern for state management pattern is built-in.

See Also

As I was writing this book, I found myself supported by the helpful folks in the ReasonML Discord Channel (*https://discord.gg/reasonml*). Language architect Cheng Lou (*https://medium.com/@chenglou*) and Jared Forsyth (*https://jaredforsyth.com/*) are both worth following as you dip into the Reason community.

Index

Symbols

react-native-elements library, 19, 66
react-native-fs package, 95
react-native-material-kit, 66
react-native-permissions, 81
react-native-progress, 23, 76
react-native-vector-icons, 69
react-native-zip-archive, 102
react-navigation, 37
react-redux, 48
React.js guide for PropTypes, 126
ReactART library, 23
Reactotron, 17
Reason, 121, 147-157
ReasonML Discord Channel, 157
red screen of death, 15
reducers, 52
Redux library
    global state management using, 47-62
    React Navigation and, 47
    redux-devtools-extension for, 17
    saving application state with, 93
    state management using, 14
redux-logger, 48, 118
redux-persist library, 94
redux-persist-filesystem-storage, 102
redux-saga, 62
redux-thunk, 62
Relay, 14
repetition, reducing, 19-22
resources, vii
routing, between login screens, 37-47
Ruby, installing, 106
runtime errors, 126-132

S

screen sizes, accommodating various, 66-69,
    112
screens, 13
SectionList, 93
semantic versioning, 106
Single Responsibility Principle, 133
Slack, 108
Snapshot tests, 133
state management
    application state, 93

global, 14
Redux library, 47-62
routing between login screens, 37-47
store metadata, 110
style and design
    animation, 76-78
    image vectors and icons, 69-76
    layouts, 66-69
    platform-specific styles, 113
    stylesheets, 63-66
stylesheets, composing, 63-66
SVG (Scalable Vector Graphics), 71
syntax transformers, 5

T

team chat services, 108
test-driven development, 138
TestFlight, 111
Tile component, 55
TileMap component, 55
type safety, 126, 147-157
TypeScript, 121, 132, 156
typographical conventions, vii

U

unit tests, 132-138
utilities, 14

V

vector editing programs, 70
version control, 15, 106
version managers, 2
views, building complex, 66-69

W

Watchman, 2

X

Xcode, 4, 23

Y

Yarn, 3, 36, 127

About the Author

Jonathan Lebensold spent his childhood playing with ribbon cables and Lego blocks. His first experience teaching others was when he was 12 years old—providing tech support to people over IRC. Later, Jonathan spent several years tapping away at a terminal, working on large information systems for Fortune 500s, nonprofits, and startups. His passion for programming blossomed when he first discovered software design patterns, test-driven development, and functional programming. Cofounding Paradem, a software consultancy, has enabled him to facilitate software and product design workshops around the world, most recently in Europe and East Africa. He spends his days taking ideas to production and helping teams architect scalable, maintainable solutions with Ruby, React, and React Native. You can find Jonathan on Twitter (*https://twitter.com/jonlebensold*), or in his kitchen perfecting his apple pie crust.

Colophon

The animal on the cover of *React Native Cookbook* is a northern goshawk (*Accipiter gentilis*), a bird of prey that is widespread throughout Eurasia and North America. It has been a popular bird in the sport of falconry for centuries, both for its speed and tendency to follow prey into thick vegetation. The name "goshawk" is derived from the Anglo-Saxon word for "goose hawk," though it is more often used to hunt rabbits, waterfowl, partridges, and pheasants. (These animals are also part of its natural diet.)

Goshawks are medium-large members of the hawk family but have proportionately large beaks and talons that provide an advantage over other raptors when hunting. Their wings are short and broad, and their tail long, both of which give them great maneuverability within their forest habitat. There are variations in color in different geographic areas, but generally, adult goshawks have orange or red eyes, blue- or brown-gray backs and wings, with a pattern of pale grey and dark bars on their bellies. Juveniles have brown plumage and yellow eyes.

Females of the species are much larger than males. Mating pairs will often use the same nest for multiple years, or at least stay in the same vicinity. It is common for the male to construct the nest, with the female supervising nearby, though she may help reinforce an older nest. These structures can be 31–47 inches long and 20–28 inches wide. Goshawks are territorial birds who will defend their hunting range and nesting site against other birds of prey, as well as goshawks of the opposite sex.

Many of the animals on O'Reilly covers are endangered; all of them are important to the world. To learn more about how you can help, go to *animals.oreilly.com*.

The cover image is from *Wood's Animate Creation*. The cover fonts are URW Typewriter and Guardian Sans. The text font is Adobe Minion Pro; the heading font is Adobe Myriad Condensed; and the code font is Dalton Maag's Ubuntu Mono.

Learn from experts.
Find the answers you need.

Sign up for a **10-day free trial** to get **unlimited access** to all of the content on Safari, including Learning Paths, interactive tutorials, and curated playlists that draw from thousands of ebooks and training videos on a wide range of topics, including data, design, DevOps, management, business—and much more.

Start your free trial at:
oreilly.com/safari

(No credit card required.)

Lightning Source UK Ltd.
Milton Keynes UK
UKOW05f1614040318

318803UK00003B/6/P